The Art of
CLEAR THINKING

The Art of
CLEAR THINKING

By **RUDOLF FLESCH**, Ph.D.

AUTHOR OF *The Art of Plain Talk*
AND *The Art of Readable Writing*

HARPER & BROTHERS PUBLISHERS NEW YORK

TO GILLIAN

CONTENTS

It would be impudent to tell intelligent, grown-up people how to think.

All I have tried to do here is to assemble certain known facts about the human mind and put them in plain English.

R. F.

A C K N O W L E D G M E N T S

I wish to thank the following persons and organizations for letting me use copyrighted material:

The New Yorker for the excerpt and illustration taken from "The Shape of a Year" by M. C. Blackman; Mr. Harry M. Callahan for his photograph, which appeared with the caption "What Is It?" in *Life*; the American Psychological Association and the *Journal of Experimental Psychology* for the chart from "An Experimental Study of the Effect of Language on the Reproduction of Visually Perceived Forms" by Carmichael, Hogan and Walter; The Journal Press and the *Journal of General Psychology* for the illustrations from "The Attainment of Concepts: I. Terminology and Methodology" by Edna Heidbreder; Oxford University Press, Inc., for the two translations of Goethe's *Wanderers Nachtlied* by Viereck and Rothensteiner appearing in *Goethe's Poems and Aphorisms*, edited by Friedrich Brun; the New York *Post* for the September 18, 1950, column "Sidewalks of New York"; the University of Chicago Press for the "Gottschaldt Figures Test," taken from *A Factorial Study of Perception* by L. L. Thurstone; Ronson Art Metal Works, Inc. and Grey Advertising Agency, Inc. for excerpts from the October 7, 1950 program of "Twenty Questions"; and Hagstrom Company Inc. for excerpts from two maps of New York City.

I am also grateful to Mr. Edmund C. Berkeley and Mr. David H. Killeffer for some very helpful ideas and suggestions.

R. F.

The Art of
CLEAR THINKING

CHAPTER 1

Robots, Apes and You

Unless we remember, we cannot understand.
— E. M. Forster, *Aspects of the Novel*

What is thinking?

Let's look for the answer in a simple case.

On December 13, 1949, Mr. Edmund Leamy, a staff writer on the New York *World-Telegram*, was engaged in a game of ticktacktoe. (In case you have forgotten or never knew how to play ticktacktoe, it goes like this: You make a field of nine squares by drawing two horizontal and two vertical lines. Then you put an X in one square, your opponent puts an O in another, and so on until one of you wins by having three marks in a row.)

In the *World-Telegram*, Mr. Leamy reported exactly how he played the game. He first put a mark in the top left-hand corner; his opponent put one in the center square. Then Mr. Leamy put a mark in the center top square; his opponent filled the top right. Whereupon Mr. Leamy picked the lower left corner, his opponent marked the left middle square, and the game was over. Mr. Leamy was stymied.

What went on in Mr. Leamy's mind while he was making his moves? Undoubtedly he was thinking. But how?

Mr. Leamy didn't describe his thought processes for the benefit of *World-Telegram* readers, but they are fairly easy to imagine—up to a point. Before he made each move, he tried to foresee his opponent's answers to various alternatives. He pictured these situations in his mind. Then he chose the move that looked most promising. Each of his decisions was based on the accumulated lessons of his lifelong experience as a ticktacktoe player.

So far, so good. Still, this is a vague description at best. It doesn't compare in exactness with Mr. Leamy's description of the actual game. We know *approximately* how the human thinking apparatus works, but when it comes to a step-by-step description of the workings of our brain cells, we can't even guess. No scientist has ever recorded the exact moves of the human brain in action.

Now let's turn from Mr. Leamy to his opponent, the ticktacktoe champion of December 13, 1949. The player's name was Mabel, and she was—and is—a machine: a ticktacktoe-playing robot invented by Mr. Robert Haufe of the California Institute of Technology. Mabel's thought processes are an open book. They are the operations of the electrical circuits Mr. Haufe built into her.

How does Mabel play her games? Easy: Mabel plays exclusively by memory, and Mabel's memory—consisting of a maze of wires and tubes —is hundred-per-cent perfect. Mabel cannot be beaten by any human player: whenever it's her move, she registers the situation facing her, matches it with one in her memory, and immediately plays what she remembers as the best move.

In fact, Mabel is so invincible a ticktacktoe player that Mr. Haufe fell to worrying that nobody might want to play games with his brain child. That's why he equipped his girl machine with an extra *imperfect-memory* circuit so that flesh-and-blood ticktacktoe enthusiasts could play with her and get more or less of an even break.

If you've kept up with the news in recent years, Mabel probably won't seem as miraculous and fantastic to you as she might have ten or twenty years ago. Today it's quite common to read and hear about the exploits of Mabel's large family of big brothers and sisters—the automatic computers or "thinking machines."

It's also quite common to read arguments about whether these machines actually think. I don't feel that it makes much difference, but I tried to find out and looked up *think* in the dictionary. There I found that to think means "to use the mind"; then I looked up *mind* and found that mind is "that which thinks." So, according to the dictionary, you can take your choice as to whether machines think or not. Practically speaking, it seems to me that Mabel was more than a match for Mr. Leamy; if *he* was thinking, it's reasonable to say *she* was too.

What makes those machines so extraordinary? From the newspaper and magazine write-ups the answer is clear: their unbelievable speed.

Take for example one of those monsters, the SEAC (Standards Eastern Automatic Computer) of the National Bureau of Standards. It was recently asked to find out whether 99,999,999,977 is a prime number—one that you can't divide by another without a remainder. That job would have taken a man with a desk calculator two full months. The machine did it in half an hour. (In case you're interested, the answer is yes.)

Or take the IBM Selective Sequence Electronic Calculator, another of those gadgets, which fills a large room in the IBM building on Madison Avenue in New York. This machine was asked to prove an abstruse theory by the Danish physicist Niels Bohr, according to which a uranium nucleus, in contrast to a drop of water, splits unevenly. A man with a desk calculator would have had to work one-and-a-half centuries on that job—yes, 150 years. The machine did it in 103 hours.

The speed of electronic thinking is literally nerve-racking. At the 1939 New York World's Fair, Westinghouse exhibited the "Nimatron," a machine that played Nim (a Chinese match game). The Nimatron behaved much like Mr. Haufe's Mabel, but the thousandth-of-a-second speed of the answers was so terrific that World's Fair visitors complained about what it did to their nervous systems. Westinghouse had to add some "delay circuits" to make the machine a little less frightening.

And yet, with all that, it isn't speed that makes these machines so superior to the human brain. It's memory. After all, there *are* human beings—lightning calculators, for instance—who can think incredibly fast. But there is no flesh-and-blood thinker whose memory, like a machine's, is always correct, always reliable, always ready. Men and women may have excellent memories but are never free of error and emotions; machines are.

Dr. Claude Shannon of Bell Telephone Laboratories, explaining the theory of an automatic chess player, lists a machine's advantages over human players this way: (1) high-speed operation; (2) freedom from errors; (3) freedom from laziness; (4) freedom from "nerves." In other words, the machine's forte, aside from speed, is an unshakable memory.

Machine memories come in all types and shapes. They may consist of electrical circuits, photographic film, magnetic tape, cathode-ray-tube surfaces, or columns of mercury. There are short-term memories for quick erasure after use, and long-term memories with a high degree of permanence. Whatever they are made of and whatever their design, they are *the* essential parts of thinking machines. As I said, there has been a lot of argument about whether mechanical brains can really be called *thinking machines.* But there is no argument whatever about their being *memory machines.*

To see exactly how a machine uses its memory, let's look at "Simple Simon," a miniature machine shown at Columbia University a few years ago. Simon was made solely for demonstration purposes; he has aptly been called the dumbest thinking machine in the world.

Simon is completely baffled when he is asked to add two and two; he can only count up to three. But when it comes to adding two and one, Simon performs splendidly and does just as well as a human being. Better, in fact: he never makes mistakes. (How many mistakes do *you* make when you have to add a row of figures?)

To do his favorite stunt of adding two and one, Simon works like this: First, he takes the number two and stores it in his memory—a set of sixteen electrical relays. Second, he takes the number one and stores *it* in his memory too. Third, he takes the idea *add* and stores *that* in his memory. Fourth, he takes these three items *out* of his memory, adds two and one, and gets three. Fifth, he stores that result in his memory. Sixth, he takes it out again and announces it to the world by flashing lights.

So you see that without a memory Simon wouldn't be a thinking machine at all, not even a dumb one; he would be just a brainless heap of hardware. In fact, Simon is as dumb as he is mainly because his memory isn't good enough; all it has room for is sixteen items.

Does all this mean that the human brain is a memory machine too? Is there really a parallel? Many people today think so. The best known computing-machine expert, Dr. Norbert Wiener of M.I.T., has written a whole book, *Cybernetics,* about this notion—adding the provocative thought that the brain work of a living human being parallels not a computing machine as such, but *one run* of such a machine. (The machine starts each new problem from scratch; man carries his past along with him till he dies.)

Some of Dr. Wiener's colleagues feel, though, that the human brain has advantages beyond the reach of the best of today's machines. Dr. Shannon, giving the human chess player his due, speaks of "the flexibility, imagination, and inductive and learning capacities of the human mind." Mr. Berkeley, the man who built Simple Simon, tells us that computers can't "do intuitive thinking, make bright guesses, and leap to conclusions." He goes on to say: "A clever wild animal, for example, a fox, can do all these things; a mechanical brain, *not yet.*"

Obviously these mathematicians feel that there is something—call it imagination, intuition, inspiration—something human beings and animals are capable of but machines are not. Machines are based on memory, and an "inspiration" is, by definition, something that comes *to* the mind—that is, from somewhere outside. Not for the machine the fanciful notion, the whimsical thought, the surprise attack on a problem. A mechanical chess player, the mathematicians insist, can be built; a mechanical poker player can't.

However, the psychology of these mathematicians is out of date. Their notions, whether they know it or not, are more than thirty years behind the times. They can be traced back to the early Gestalt psychologists and their famous discovery of "insight."

Let's see how it all started. Let's go back to March 11, 1914, to the island of Tenerife in the Atlantic. There Dr. Wolfgang Köhler, the German psychologist, is beginning his stick experiments with chimpanzees. Nueva, a homely but smart young girl chimpanzee, is sitting in her cage. Inside the cage is a stick. Now Dr. Köhler puts some bananas outside the cage, beyond her reach. She tries to get at the fruit, can't do it and is unhappy. Seven minutes pass while she moans and whimpers. Then suddenly she looks at the stick, stops moaning, grabs the stick, reaches out and pulls in the bananas.

What has happened? Obviously, something suddenly clicked in Nueva's brain. Dr. Köhler, in his book *The Mentality of Apes*, puts it down as "insight." Here's something that doesn't seem explicable by the simple operation of memory.

Since 1914, thousands of experiments have proved that insight is a reality. But where does it come from? Does it pop into the mind from nowhere or can it be traced back to memory, after all? In the thirties and forties, psychologists began to tackle the *sources* of insight. On that March day in 1914, they said, Nueva had been just three days out of the jungle, having spent there some four to seven years. What happened during all these years? Did she play with sticks? Did she reach for out-of-the-way bananas? Did she ever stumble on the great stick-banana secret? Since they couldn't bring back the dim past of Köhler's apes, the psychologists started new experiments—this time beginning long before the moment of sudden "inspiration."

The clearest evidence comes from experiments carried out in 1944 by Dr. Herbert G. Birch at the Yerkes Laboratories of Primate Biology at Orange Park, Florida. Dr. Birch didn't take any chances with apes who had roamed the jungle for years. *His* chimpanzees were a highly select crew, the nearest thing he could come to animals produced in test tubes.

In his scientific report, Dr. Birch introduces us to six extremely well-brought-up chimpanzees. Four are boys—Alf, Bard, Ken and Art—and two are girls—Jenny and Jojo. All of them were born in the laboratories and scientifically raised in the nursery ever since they were two weeks old. Complete diaries were kept about their weights, eating habits, first teeth, behavior at games and temper tantrums.

Every day, Alf, Bard, Ken, Art, Jenny and Jojo play together in a nice enclosed play yard. They have a big tree and a slide, and life is a lot of fun.

The years go by, and now they are all between four and five years old. The big day arrives. They are put in a cage, and Dr. Birch gives them essentially the same tests Dr. Köhler gave his apes thirty years before. There they are, sitting in a cage that contains a stick. Outside, beyond reach, is some food.

Dr. Birch, notebook in hand, watches and waits for the moment of insight. Each animal is given half an hour for the test. Will they pull in the food with the stick?

The answer is no in the cases of Alf, Ken, Jenny and Art. First they try to reach the food. Then, when this doesn't work, they beg Dr. Birch to hand it to them, but he refuses. Ken, Jenny and Art get so mad they grab the stick and throw it in a corner. Alf doesn't, though. He disregards the stick and just sulks.

But when it's time for Jojo to take the test, things are different. Jojo enters the cage, goes to the grill, looks at the food outside, glances at the stick, picks it up immediately and pulls in the food, just so. Then she lays the stick on the table, picks up the food by hand and settles down to eating. Time spent: twelve seconds.

What makes Jojo different? Superior intellect? Inspiration? Dr. Birch goes to his records and finds out. Sure enough: "Jojo has made a regular practice of stick-using, and on numerous occasions has been observed to reach through the mesh of her indoor cage and flick the electric light switch off and on with a stick. She has developed, also, the further habit of unscrewing an electric light bulb by reaching through her cage-mesh with a stick." In other words, Jojo is an inveterate stick-user. None of the others has ever been observed reaching out with a stick—not to speak of such shenanigans as turning off lights or unscrewing bulbs.

But Jojo isn't the most interesting case of the six; it's Bard. With him, Dr. Birch has the rare privilege of being an eyewitness at the birth of an idea. When Bard comes into the cage, he first behaves like all the others except Jojo. He reaches for the food, begs Dr. Birch to give it to him, then wanders about the cage, begs again, but it's no use. He has used up four minutes of his half hour. Once again he reaches out for the food, and this time his thrashing arm brushes against the stick and moves it accidentally about three inches. The stick pivots and the other end sweeps the food a little nearer to one side. Bard stops. He looks carefully at the situation. Then he gently shoves the stick, watches the food, sees that it moves, shoves the stick some more and finally pulls in the food.

Bard is happy and eats. Dr. Birch is happy too. He has tracked down that mysterious thing, insight. He has watched what happened to Bard in the cage and knows that there must have been a similar moment in the life of Dr. Köhler's Nueva while she was cavorting in the jungle. Problems are solved by insight, yes. But there's no insight that doesn't go back to some actual experience sometime, somewhere.

To prove Dr. Birch's point once and for all, the six chimpanzees get three more days in the play yard before they return to the test cage. Now the play yard is well equipped with sticks, and the animals play with them to their heart's desire. On the third day, the use of sticks as tools is old hat to all of them. They amuse themselves by poking at Dr. Birch through the enclosure mesh. Art has become a great nuisance: the others complain that he threatens them with his stick all the time.

On the fourth day, they go back to the test cage and perform beautifully. Now they all just look at the situation, pull in the food and eat. Jojo now takes five seconds all in all, but even Alf, the slowest, does it in one-third of a minute.

Where does all this leave such things as intuition, bright guesses, leaping to conclusions—the things that Mr. Berkeley says mechanical brains "can not yet do"? It reduces them to the application of experience and memory. It shows that, in theory at least, a machine could be built that learns by registering experience and matches the registered experience with new problem situations. This sounds fantastic, but the mathematicians are already talking about it. For instance, the British mathematician Dr. Bronowski recently described an automatic chess player that would learn from experience and get better and better as it goes along.

So the gap is narrowing: the animals' insight can be traced back to memory and the robots may eventually be trained to solve problems by insight.

Midway between the ape brain and the machine brain is the one you carry in your head. It's a reasonable guess that it works similarly to the other two—those two brains science has shown to be so much alike. If so, it's proper to call your brain a memory machine; what you do—whether you play a game of canasta or write The Great American Novel—is to solve problems by the application of past experience.

So here is your definition of thinking: It is the manipulation of memories.

CHAPTER 2

Nerves and Thoughts

To me as a physiologist . . . the evidence appears to be strong that mind or consciousness is associated with a limited but shifting area of integrated activity in the cortex of the brain.

— Walter B. Cannon, *The Way of an Investigator*

The "Third Programme" of the B.B.C. (the British government-run radio network) is famous for being the most highbrow program on the world's air waves. In 1949 it set some sort of record: it offered its listeners a lecture series on "the physical basis of mind" by no less than ten brain experts and philosophers, including two Nobel prize winners. Whether the series was successful as radio entertainment, I don't know; at any rate, it came up with some interesting answers to what must be the oldest philosophical question in the world.

There was a difference of opinion, of course. Some of the lecturers felt that mind and body were entirely separate, others thought they were two sides of the same thing. On the whole, the materialists seemed to have the edge. Professor Gilbert Ryle, an Oxford philosopher, summed up their views by telling a story about the peasant who had never seen a locomotive. Somebody explained to him how a steam engine works. "Yes," the peasant answered, "I quite understand. But there is really a horse inside, isn't there?" So the peasant was asked to examine the engine and peep into every crevice of it. When he couldn't find any horse inside, he still had an answer. "I know," he said. "It's an *invisible* horse."

This, Professor Ryle said, is the attitude of people who insist there

9

must be an invisible thing called mind inside the body. Let's stop looking for the horse, he suggested, and find out all we can about the engine.

The one man who has perhaps done most in exploring the mind's engine—the human brain—was one of the ten lecturers. He is Dr. Wilder Penfield, Professor of Neurology and Neurosurgery at McGill University in Montreal. During the past fifteen years, Dr. Penfield has performed hundreds of operations on tumors and other diseases of the brain. But not content with trying to help his patients, he used his access to all these exposed brains to assemble a body of priceless information. Thanks to him and his fellow researchers, we now have a fairly accurate map of the human brain.

Mapping the brain is not a new thing by any means. It has been going on ever since Dr. Paul Broca, a Frenchman, localized the speech center in 1861. But Dr. Penfield did something entirely new. He applied a wire (with a very weak electrical current) to various areas of the brain and made his patients, in turn, move their arms or legs, utter sounds, hear noises, or see shapes and colors. The patients, under local anesthesia, did all these things without wanting to, compelled by the electrical stimulation of the appropriate brain cells. If you want to raise your right arm, you activate certain nerve cells in your brain, and up goes your arm. Dr. Penfield is the first man in history who did this "mental operation" from the outside. And the patients' arms went up.

But Dr. Penfield did even more. For instance, he established beyond any doubt that the brain has two parallel halves and that most of the important brain centers exist in duplicate, one right and one left. The connecting nerves cross from one side of the body to the other. So most of us who are right-handed are left-brained and speak, listen and think with the left side of our brain only.

On top of all that, Dr. Penfield was able to tap people's memories with his little electrical gadget. It turned out that the memory of right-handed people is located in the left temporal lobe of the brain, behind the temple and above the ear. (Or rather, that memory is located in the whole brain but activated from that particular area.)

When Dr. Penfield touched that area of the brain of one patient—she was a fourteen-year-old girl—she cried out: "Oh, I can see something coming at me! My mother and my brothers are yelling at me for doing something wrong! Stop them!"

When the memory center of another young girl was tapped, she said: "A dream is starting. . . . There are a lot of people in the living room. . . . I think one of them is my mother."

Another of the patients was a fourteen-year-old school boy. When the electrical wire was applied to his memory nerves, he exclaimed: "I see two men sitting in an armchair." When another spot nearby was touched, he said: "I see a man fighting."

A young clergyman's memory area produced this: "Wait! I feel like I'm going away—and I see my mother again. She's singing her lullaby now. Listen! 'Hushaby, my baby . . .'"

Summarizing these and many other experiments, Dr. Penfield says:

> The music a patient hears or the appearance before him of his mother or friend are memories. . . . In some way the stimulating electrode is activating acquired patterns of nerve cell connection which are involved in the mechanism of memory. . . . Now, if the individual were to recall, voluntarily, the appearance of his mother's living room, we may surmise that he would activate the same pattern of nerve cell connections. But he would be activating it *from within*.

And how do you activate your memory nerve cells from within? Why, you do it electrically, just as Dr. Penfield did it from the outside. This has been known ever since Dr. Hans Berger of Jena, Germany, started the study of electrical brain currents in 1928. In the years since, the recording of electrical brain waves has become routine.

But until recently, researchers hadn't found out a lot about the electrical stimulation of memories. The normal rhythm of the brain waves is the so-called alpha rhythm, and that goes on pretty steadily and regularly as long as your brain does nothing in particular—when it "idles." As soon as you start thinking hard or try to remember something, the alpha waves stop.

Then, in 1949, Dr. John L. Kennedy of Tufts College, Massachusetts, came upon something new. He was doing a study of eye movements in reading and was running a routine brain wave record. But there was a disturbance in the record and gradually he realized that he had unearthed a new and different kind of brain wave. He decided to call them kappa waves.

Kappa waves appeared on Dr. Kennedy's recording machines when he gave his test students arithmetic problems and geometrical puzzles, or asked them to remember the names of the forty-eight states. Once he and his associates decided to hitch their instrument to an electrical oscillator so that the kappa waves would produce a noise instead of moving a pen. Then they asked a test student to "keep adding twenty-sevens orally." The result was a record on which a brain whistled while it worked: "Twenty-seven. (Pause.) Tweet! Fifty-four. (Longer pause.) Tweet! Eighty-one."

Dr. Kennedy concluded that kappa waves are connected with the effort to remember—with the conscious electrical operation of the memory. They are a sign of the groping of the mind—"sand in the gears."

And from what part of the brain do you think Dr. Kennedy picked up his kappa waves? Yes, you guessed it: behind the temple, on the left side—exactly where Dr. Penfield was able to turn on memories from the outside.

But, you may say, all this concerns only a rather minor sort of thinking. Dreams, memories of childhood, arithmetical problems, the forty-eight states—what does all this amount to? Thinking that matters is about important things—man and his future, freedom and responsibility, good and evil. Deep thinking, you say, cannot be tackled by surgery and research instruments.

But it can and it has been. Which brings us back once more to chimpanzees. This time the story is about two Connecticut chimpanzees, Becky and Lucy, who lived at the physiological laboratory at Yale. Two doctors, John F. Fulton and Carlyle Jacobsen, brought them up with all the proper laboratory ape training. They passed all intelligence tests splendidly. After half a year, in June, 1934, the doctors performed an experimental operation on both animals, removing the entire prefrontal region of their brains—the part that lies behind the forehead. Then Becky and Lucy went through a new series of tests. They did all right, but with one tremendous difference: they just didn't seem to care about the outcome. Before the operation they had thrown a tantrum as soon as they had made the wrong choice and didn't get the food reward. Now, when they made a wrong choice, "they just shrugged their shoulders and went on doing something else."

Fulton and Jacobsen reported their experiment at a London medical convention in 1935. There Dr. Egaz Moniz, a neurologist from Lisbon, heard them, went home, got together with a surgeon, Dr. Almeida Lima, and began to perform similar operations on mental patients. But instead of cutting off the prefrontal region altogether, they got the same effect by cutting the nerve connections between that region and the thalamus —the deep inside part of the brain that is said to be the seat of the emotions. This operation is called prefrontal lobotomy (leucotomy in England). In October, 1949, it brought Dr. Moniz the Nobel prize.

As I am writing (January, 1951), prefrontal lobotomy has been performed on over 20,000 people. It has been extraordinarily successful in freeing mental sufferers from anxiety, phobias, delusions, persecution complexes and epileptic fits. It has been used to relieve patients with organic diseases of unbearable pain. But it has also produced changes in the patients' personalities somewhat like the changes in the personalities of Becky and Lucy. It has changed most of the 20,000 cases into different people.

After lobotomy, the wife of one patient said: "Doctor, you have given me a new husband. He isn't the same man."

The mother of another patient said: "She is my daughter but yet a different person. She is with me in body but her soul is in some way lost. Those deep feelings, the tenderness, are gone. She is hard, somehow."

The friend of a third patient said: "I'm living now with another person. She is shallow in some way."

The wife of a fourth said: "I have lost my husband. I'm alone. I must take over all responsibilities now."

Two English doctors reported on a number of similar cases. One patient continued to lead his normal life but lost all relationship with even the closest members of his family and showed no interest whatever in his children. Another seemed to exist in a kind of vacuum; no friendship was possible with him. A third, a skilled mechanic still considered an excellent craftsman, lost the ability to undertake complicated jobs. He stopped studying and seemed to have resigned himself to being a routine worker. An unemployed clergyman didn't seem in the least concerned that he was out of work. He left all decisions to his wife and was completely passive when it came to planning for the future.

A Swedish doctor reported the case of another clergyman who had undergone a lobotomy operation. He become addicted to sudden rages and crying spells, couldn't concentrate, and ignored responsibilities. When invited to preach he pieced together an old sermon.

And Dr. Penfield in his book on the brain describes the case of his own sister, whose frontal lobe had been removed. Dr. Penfield watched her in her home, "supervising her six children, talking and laughing at the dinner table, perfectly normally, as she would have done ten years earlier. She had not forgotten how to cook, but she had lost the capacity of planning and preparing a meal alone."

Dr. Penfield concludes that the operation had impaired "those mental processes which are prerequisite to planned initiative." Another doctor summed up the effects of lobotomy this way: "The patients understand ethical problems but they fail to apply it to themselves. They lose the capacity to understand the objectivity of the concept moral."

Drs. Walter Freeman and James W. Watts, two leading specialists in this field, say flatly: "It is becoming more and more plain that patients who undergo lobotomy must sacrifice some of the virtues, some of the driving force, some of the uplift, altruism, creative spirit, soul or whatever else one would like to call it."

Work is going on to refine the operation in such a way that the patient is cured without changes in his personality. But it is pretty clear by now that lobotomy has shown us that area of the brain (behind the forehead) that is the center of planning, moral responsibility, initiative, imagination—the highest kind of thinking man can do.

And so surgery and neurological research are now pointing to the thalamus as the seat of the emotions, to the frontal lobe as the seat of the moral sense, and to the rest of the brain as the seat of man's general conscious self. When Sigmund Freud, years ago, divided the mind into the ego (the conscious self), the id (the unconscious drives) and the superego (the moral censor of our actions), most people considered it a grand metaphor; maybe he did himself. Yet today the same division shows up in the nerve cells of people's brains.

What does all this tell you about thinking? It tells you that thinking is closely connected with the activity of certain specific nerve cells in your brain—or, if you care to put it this way, that it *is* the activity of certain nerve cells. Just exactly how the nerve cells work when you are thinking, nobody knows. But there's no question that they do somehow, and scientists have come forth with a goodly number of theories to explain the mystery.

First of all, they are all agreed that a thought, an idea, a memory corresponds to a pattern of nerve cells—and since the number of your brain cells is estimated as ten or twelve billion, the number of possible patterns is astronomical.

From there on, the theories differ. The older notion was that these patterns were fixed—memories etched in your brain, so to speak. But this is out of date. Now scientists prefer to talk of "reverberations" or "attunements" and use such images as a musical key or the rippling waves in a pond.

And that's as far as science goes today. We know that when you try to think of a hippopotamus, your brain doesn't produce anything like a composite photograph of all hippopotami you've known; instead, it supplies you with a pattern of nerve cells that symbolically, in your system of thinking, stands for hippopotamus.

Nobody has observed this process, but that doesn't mean that nobody will. As you have seen, the discoveries described in this chapter are all pretty new; the earliest, the study of electrical brain waves, started in 1928. So it's not only possible, it is probable that scientists will soon find the key to that great riddle, the physiology of thought. The discovery may come gradually, from the combined work of many researchers, or suddenly, from the mind of one. Whenever it comes, it will be one of the greatest landmarks of science.

Most people seem to feel that the twentieth century will go down in scientific history as the century that brought us atomic energy. My hunch is that it will be known as the century when the gap between mind and matter was finally bridged.

CHAPTER 3

Do You See What I See?

People don't use their eyes. They never see a bird, they see a sparrow. They never see a tree, they see a birch. They see concepts.

—Joyce Cary

Bernard Shaw, who considered himself a teacher rather than an entertainer, always insisted that he wrote his plays so that people would read his prefaces. There, in the prefaces, is the theory behind the action on the stage. How, for instance, does Shaw account for Saint Joan's visions? The preface has the answer:

Joan was what Francis Galton and other modern investigators of human faculty call a visualizer. She saw imaginary saints just as some other people see imaginary diagrams and landscapes with numbers dotted about them, and are thereby able to perform feats of memory and arithmetic impossible to non-visualizers.

Now who was Francis Galton and what is a visualizer? The answer makes rather an interesting story.

Sir Francis Galton was a nineteenth-century scientific jack-of-all-trades, a cousin of Charles Darwin, an explorer, meteorologist, anthropologist, and psychologist, the founder of the science of eugenics, and the man who is responsible for the general use of fingerprinting. In 1883 he published a book, *Inquiries into Human Faculty and Its Development*—a grand hodgepodge of miscellaneous fascinating information, from a description of a high-pitched dog-whistle Galton invented to a poker-faced statistical study of the efficacy of prayer, particularly in the case of monarchs stricken with illness. Among all these things, the book contained a long section on "mental imagery," the first study of this kind anybody had ever done.

What Galton was after was very simple. He wanted to know what kind of pictures people carried in their heads, and so he wrote to a number of his scientific friends and asked what they saw when they thought of an object. ("Suppose it is your breakfast table as you sat down to it this morning.")

The results of this survey flabbergasted Galton. Most of his friends wrote back that they didn't see a thing and asked what in the world he was talking about.

After this complete letdown by his fellow scientists, the bewildered Galton turned to "persons whom I met in general society." They made him feel much better.

Many men and a yet larger number of women, and many boys and girls, declared that they habitually saw mental imagery, and that it was perfectly distinct to them and full of colour. . . . They described their imagery in minute detail, and they spoke in a tone of surprise at my apparent hesitation in accepting what they said. . . . Reassured by this happier experience I recommended to inquire among scientific men, and soon found scattered instances of what I sought. . . .

After some more research, Galton found that pictures in the mind's eye are quite common among most people, but highly uncommon among scientists and abstract thinkers in general. He concluded that deep thinkers consider mental pictures a nuisance and get rid of all this imagery by disuse.

But Galton didn't stop at collecting mental pictures of breakfast tables. While he was at it, he also asked people how they saw numbers, the days of the week, the months of the year and the alphabet.

The answers he got make a weird collection. For instance, look at some of his "Examples of Number-Forms" on the next page—abstract drawings that seem to make neither rhyme nor reason. But that's what people said they had in their heads, and there is no question that lots of them did and do. (Galton says "the peculiarity in question is found in about one out of every thirty adult males or fifteen females.")

In fact, even these odd drawings are rather mild examples of "number-forms." They don't compare, for instance, with the system used by Sir Flinders Petrie, the famous archaeologist. Petrie calmly informed Galton that he habitually worked out sums with an imaginary slide rule. He simply set it the desired way and mentally read off the result.

Examples of Number-Forms.

Many people told Galton about complicated color schemes connected with these number-forms. Some "saw" the letters of the alphabet in a certain way; others turned in reports on how the days of the week looked to them. One woman wrote: "When I think of Wednesday, I see a kind of oval flat wash of yellow emerald green; for Tuesday, a gray sky colour; for Thursday, a brown-red irregular polygon; and a dull yellow smudge for Friday."

The months of the year [Galton wrote], are usually perceived as ovals, and they as often follow one another in a reverse direction to those of the figures on the clock, as in the same direction. It is a common peculiarity that the months do not occupy equal spaces, but those that are most important to the child extend more widely than the rest. There are many varieties as to the topmost month; it is by no means always January.

All these discoveries of Galton have been proved many times since; in fact, mental imagery has been rediscovered several times by people who had never heard of his book. A recent, highly amusing example is an article called "The Shape of a Year" by M. C. Blackman, which appeared in *The New Yorker* in 1948.* Mr. Blackman explained that in his mind a year looked like this:

He goes on to say:

My visualized year is an elongated oval, flat on one side and with one end larger than the other, like a childish drawing of an egg, or like a malformed race track, lying lengthwise from east to west. January and winter both start in the southeast corner of my year, and never mind those odd days in December that the solstice appends to winter like an ungainly prefix. January, February, and March head westward in a straight line. They are uniformly rather long months and they are gray. (I forgot to say that my envisioned year has color.)

April, May, and June whip around a sharp curve at the little, or western, end of the egg in a gentle riot of pastel that begins with pale yellow and ends in a dark and dusty green. These are short and dizzying months, all

* Text and illustrations by M. C. Blackman. Reprinted by permission. Copyright 1948 *The New Yorker* Magazine, Inc.

of them together covering little more distance than any one of the winter months.

Now we are heading eastward in a long, sagging curve that is divided into the two months of July and August. These constitute summer. Both are very long, but August is a little longer than July, and their sandy hue is almost as drab as winter's gray.

At the northeast corner, there is a rather sharp turn into the fall, which is four months long and heads almost straight south to January, and the beginning of a new year. The months of September, October, November, and December are short, snappy months and as colorful as a kaleidoscope, except that December begins to gray a trifle the week after Christmas.

All this will seem strange to you if you are one of the majority of nonvisualizers—or familiar if you are a visualizer like me. (My year is a little like Mr. Blackman's, only it stands miraculously on the tip of the oval; also it's black and white, since I am color-blind.) At any rate, what does all this show about the way people think?

It seems to me that it shows a great deal. Surely, the visualizers are not a race apart; their memories are patterns of nerve cells just like everybody else's. The difference is only that they feel their patterns visually rather than some other way, and so are able to show others what they look like. The abstract thinker may have just as rigidly fixed patterns in *his* mind, but since they are not visual, he has no way of conveying their shape to anyone else. But both of them think with patterns. When they think of a number, they put it in its proper place in their mental number pattern; when they think of a date, they mark it on their mental calendar.

The visualizers have given us some vivid examples of how this process works. Take the case of Mr. Salo Finkelstein, the famous lightning calculator who could add three- and four-place numbers faster than an adding machine and could, in one minute, analyze any four-place number into the sum of four squares. He told psychologists that he saw all numbers he worked with clearly as if they were written with chalk on a blackboard in his own handwriting, about two to three inches high and at a distance of about fourteen to sixteen inches from the eyes. Another lightning calculator, Diamondi, saw all numbers "as if they were photographed." (A third, Inandi, was an auditory type and didn't see a thing.) Or take Mr. Jean-Francois Rozan, the wonder boy among the fabulous UN simultaneous interpreters. "I have a ticker tape in my mind," he says. "It moves past the back of my eyes, and on it are the words I hear. So even if I fall behind on a speech, I can always read back and catch up."

All this sounds very wonderful. It gives us a glimpse of the way a miraculous memory works, and shows us that the memory of ordinary mortals works in similar fashion: by filing impressions away in set patterns. But there's a drawback to this: the habit of remembering things in set patterns is apt to distort them.

The British psychologist, Mr. F. C. Bartlett, wrote a fat book called *Remembering*, in which he showed clearly by innumerable experiments that we hardly ever remember things the way they are; we remember them the way we think they *should have been*. By what Mr. Bartlett calls "effort after meaning," we work on our memories until they conveniently fit the patterns we already have in our minds. "Remembering," Mr. Bartlett concludes, "is an imaginative reconstruction or construction. . . . It is hardly ever exact."

In other words, as soon as we *try* to remember, distortion creeps in and we are apt to recall something that wasn't so. Marcel Proust, the famous author of *Remembrance of Things Past*, knew this very well. He wanted to create a picture of true memories. Therefore he never let his characters remember deliberately, and his great novel is a mosaic of what he called "involuntary memories"—the kind that stir in the mind when you taste a once-familiar taste or hear a long-forgotten melody. "Involuntary memories," Proust wrote to a friend, "alone have the stamp of authenticity."

But as if the distortion of memories wasn't enough, the patterns in our minds distort our experience to begin with—at the very moment of perception. Not only is it almost impossible to remember exactly, it is hard to *see, hear* and *feel* exactly. Perception isn't a matter of the senses only. We don't see just with our eyes. We also see with our brain.

A few years ago this fact was dramatized by some ingenious apparatus rigged up by Mr. Adelbert Ames of the Hanover Institute in New Hampshire. Unsuspecting visitors were asked to look at an object through a peephole. What they saw was a chair. At least they thought it was a chair; they could have sworn it was a chair. But it wasn't: it was a combination of some sticks, arranged so that it fitted exactly the pattern *chair* in the mind of everybody who looked through the peephole.

Not content with that, Mr. Ames also rigged up an illusionary room—a sort of torture chamber for the human mind. Looking into that room through another peephole, the victim would see a giant in one corner and a dwarf in another; then the two would change places and the dwarf would be a giant and the giant a dwarf. People would walk around to the back of the magic room, see how the thing was set up, and return to the peephole. But it was no use: their mind played them the same trick again, in spite of the fact that now they *knew*.

All of which goes to show that your mind doesn't register what's in front of your eyes; it's your eyes that register what's in the back of your mind. This may be confusing and irritating to you, but it's tremendously useful to psychologists. They have explored the patterns in people's minds by all sorts of "projective" tests, all built on the principle of showing people something ambiguous and asking them: "What do you see in this?"

Projective tests are based on inkblots, pictures, and story situations. I thought of showing you here one of the inkblots from the Rorschach Test. But then I ran across a picture in *Life* entitled "What is it?" that seemed a more interesting illustration of the same idea. Look at it on the next page. What do you see?

Or look at the series of pictures on the following page. They show the results of an interesting experiment. People were asked to look at the figures in the center column and reproduce them immediately afterward from memory. However, to one-half of the group the pictures were announced with the words on Word List I, and to the other half with those on Word List II. Result: Two-thirds distorted the pictures one way or the other. The right and left columns show typical examples of their handiwork.

Another experiment was run at Harvard during World War II in connection with the study of rumor. People were shown a series of pictures and asked to report in detail what they saw. They promptly reported all details as they thought they should have been rather than as they were. A sign that showed a distance in kilometers was changed into one that showed miles. A movie marquee reading GENE ANTRY was invariably remembered as GENE AUTRY. A drugstore in the middle of a block moved up and became a "corner drugstore." A Red Cross truck loaded with explosives changed into one carrying medical supplies. A razor in the hand of a white man arguing with a Negro switched to the hand of the Negro.

Still another experiment had to do with the size of money. A group of Boston school children were asked to estimate the size of coins, from a penny to a half-dollar. (They used a gadget with a little lighted circle they could change in size.) It turned out that *all children overrated*

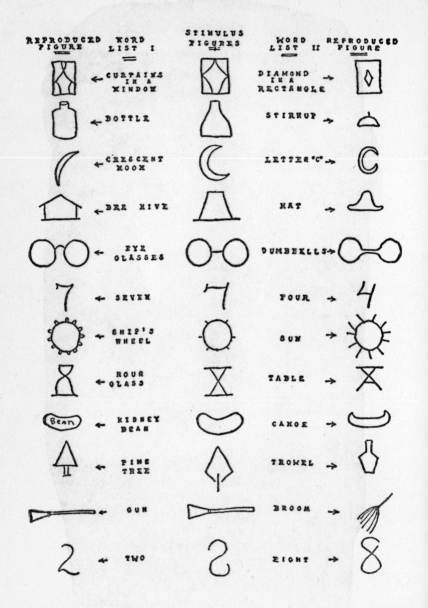

REPRODUCED FIGURE	WORD LIST I	STIMULUS FIGURES	WORD LIST II	REPRODUCED FIGURE
	← CURTAINS IN A WINDOW		DIAMOND IN A RECTANGLE →	
	← BOTTLE		STIRRUP →	
	← CRESCENT MOON		LETTER "C" →	
	← BEE HIVE		HAT →	
	← EYE GLASSES		DUMBELLS →	
	← SEVEN		FOUR →	
	← SHIP'S WHEEL		SUN →	
	← HOUR GLASS		TABLE →	
	← KIDNEY BEAN		CANOE →	
	← PINE TREE		TROWEL →	
	← GUN		BROOM →	
	← TWO		EIGHT →	

the size of all coins. But the experimenters went one step further: they compared children from a settlement house in a Boston slum with those from a progressive school in a swanky suburb. They found, in cold statistics, that when slum children instead of young suburbanites looked at money, the dimes, quarters, and half-dollars invariably grew one-third bigger.

So what you see depends almost as much on you as on the object. Perception is a key to your personality. What did you see in the picture from *Life* on page 23? It bore the following caption:

Visitors to New York's Museum of Modern Art have been puzzling for weeks over this beautiful picture by Harry Callahan, a Chicago photographer. Some guesses: tree stump, black cat, ink spot. Answer: it is a simple silhouette of a nude from the waist up, her arms over her head.

What goes for pictures goes for stories, situations, any kind of experience. A situation in itself has no meaning; it all depends on who is looking at it. Twenty years ago, a group of well-known English writers furnished a perfect demonstration of this fact. There were fourteen of them, and each agreed to write a story based on the same plot. The plot was furnished by Mr. John Fothergill, a literary innkeeper near Oxford, and it ran like this:

A man gets into correspondence with a woman whom he doesn't know and he finds romance in it. Then he sees a girl, falls in love with her in the ordinary way, marries her and drops the academic correspondence. Happiness, then friction. He writes again to the unknown woman and finds consolation till by an accident it is discovered that the married couple are writing to one another.

Reading the fourteen stories, you have to remind yourself again and again that the plot is actually the same. Rebecca West deals with the struggles of a man who grew up in a family of fake spiritual mediums; G. K. Chesterton writes a moral tale to show the value of humility; Storm Jameson chooses as her main theme the psychological problems of a young Jew; Frank Swinnerton comes up with a humorous story of two cockney types full of romantic nonsense; Margaret Kennedy describes the revolt of an emancipated mid-Victorian housewife; and so it goes.

After all, what is a plot? What are facts? Your mind meets them for a fleeting moment and immediately proceeds to make them over in your image.

There is a little book on my shelves that contains a set of rules for thinking. Rule Number One reads: "Define the primary facts in connection with your observation, and separate these facts from any opinions or impressions."

An excellent rule—except for one little thing: it can't be done.

CHAPTER 4

Of Thingummies and Whatchamacallits

His hearers were frankly incredulous. They pointed out that the friend-ship between the two artistes had always been a byword or whatever you called it. A well-read Egg summed it up by saying that they were like Thingummy and What's-his-name.

—P. G. Wodehouse, *The Crime Wave at Blandings*

The most famous sentence in William James' most famous book, *Principles of Psychology,* is this: "A polyp would be a conceptual thinker if a feeling of 'Hollo! thingumbob again!' ever flitted through his mind."

James is talking about our concepts, or general ideas. What he means is that we think in concepts as soon as we realize that two experiences have something in common. The basis of all concepts, he says, is the sense of sameness.

Looked at this way, a concept doesn't sound like anything very glamorous or exciting. And yet, philosophers have been getting excited over concepts—or universals, as they call them—for over two thousand years. Ever since Plato and Socrates, they have considered universals as more important than anything else.

As you can imagine, William James had little patience with this sort of thing. Shortly after the thingumbob sentence he writes: "The over-whelming and portentous character ascribed to universal conceptions is surprising. . . . The traditional universal-worship can only be called a bit of perverse sentimentalism."

Today practically all psychologists—and most philosophers too—agree with William James. They wouldn't think of worshiping universals. In fact, they consider it simply routine to produce concepts whenever necessary in the psychological research laboratory.

To do that, they use such research tools as card-sorting games and nonsense syllables. For instance, in a recent experiment, people were shown, among others, the following figures:

Each of these figures was announced with the word *pran*. Naturally, it didn't take anybody very long to catch on to the fact that this is a *pran:*

Obviously, what happened was simply that by the time a person got to the candy sticks, it dawned on him that the pattern was the same as that of the flowers and he said to himself: "So that's what *pran* means! Why, it's ✗ !"

Or, to take a different example, I once met a girl who said emphatically that she'd never marry a Brooklyn dentist. (I am not making this up; you can't make up things like that.)

The girl explained her remark by recounting sundry experiences in dating Brooklyn dentists. She felt that she was perfectly justified in drawing her general conclusion.

Now the girl arrived at her concept of *Brooklyn dentist* exactly the same way the people in the laboratory arrived at the concept of *pran.* She first met, say, Charlie, who was tall, dark and handsome and, among other things, a Brooklyn dentist. No concept yet. Next she dated George, who had red hair and wore glasses and, it so happened, was also a Brooklyn dentist. Still no concept. Then she dated Peter, who was fat, bald and brilliant. He too, it turned out, was a Brooklyn dentist. Suddenly it dawned on her that there was something the three boys had in common: their pattern of behavior, their line, their general outlook on life—something. Thinking back, she recognized ✗ in all three boys: the concept of *Brooklyn dentist* had been formed.

The standard example in the psychology textbooks is, of course, a little different. It deals with a child forming the concept of a dog. The child meets Fido and the grownups tell him that this is a dog. Then he comes up against Rex and this too, he is told, is a dog. Finally the child makes the acquaintance of Rover, another so-called dog, and so on. Gradually he gets to know what a dog is.

This is all right, as far as it goes, but the general impression is wrong.

In the first place, you get the idea that the sheer accumulation of similar experiences will produce a concept. It won't. It won't, that is, unless after the second or third or fourth experience, you take, in your mind, another look at the thing you saw originally. Otherwise you may experience the same thing a hundred times and still form no concept. In other words, a concept is the product of hindsight, of focusing on something you didn't pay attention to originally.

The dog example is also misleading in other ways. For one thing, it stresses the visual memory. At least, you get the notion that the dog concept is a composite *picture* of Fido, Rex and Rover. Actually, the thing is of course much more complex. Maybe the three dogs don't look very much alike: but they bark, they behave in similar fashion, they *feel* sort of similar. The dog concept, like most of our concepts, is not two-dimensional or even three-dimensional. It's a complex pattern of sights, sounds, smells, tastes, feelings and other sensations and impressions that are hard to put into words. What are the elements that go into such a concept as *Brooklyn dentist?* Figure it out for yourself.

The dog concept may also give you a wrong notion of what corresponds to a concept in the brain. Of course, as I said before, nobody knows yet what goes on in the brain when we think. But it's possible to form theories about it, and the scientists' theory is definitely *not* that the concept *dog* is simply the memories of Rex, Fido and Rover, super-imposed upon one another. The concept *dog*, they say, is a pattern of a dog in the abstract, a combination of doggish features and qualities.

Now the interesting question is, How do we recognize a dog when we see one? Obviously we match the sense impression of the animal we see against the multidimensional nerve cell pattern *dog* in our brain. But exactly how do we do this? The mathematicians and neurologists have come up with a fascinating theory to answer this question.

They say that the brain operates like radar or television: it continually "scans" the field. The basic piece of equipment in radar or television is a "scanner" that sweeps a beam rhythmically back and forth over the field. In the same way, the theory goes, the brain uses a rhythmic scanning beam to match a new experience against its patterns of general concepts. And what is that rhythmic electrical scanning beam? Why, the theorists have a beautiful answer to that one: it's our old friend, the alpha rhythm of the brain waves.

Whether all this is so, I don't know. But it does sound like a plausible theory and, at any rate, it's helpful to remember whenever you get confused as to what a concept is and how it works.

And now let me talk about the thing that's *really* confusing about the famous child-dog example. When you look at it closely, you'll find that the child isn't forming a concept at all: he is only learning—from the grownups—a concept that has already been formed millions of years ago. The child who adds the familiar concept *dog* to his store of knowledge is one thing: the girl who, by her own experience, arrives at the brand-new concept *Brooklyn dentist* is something altogether different.

For the person who wants to learn how to think better, the important thing about concepts is just this: that they are not powerful invisible somethings floating somewhere in outer space, but simply nerve patterns in our brains that were formed at a certain time after we were exposed to certain experiences. If we want to fix this point clearly in our minds, the worst thing we can do is to look at a child learning a familiar concept. In such a situation the concept looks as if it had existed from time immemorial; next to it, the child's brain looks pretty small and insignificant. The picture is all wrong.

To get rid of this optical illusion, let's look at some examples of how concepts were actually born—that is, formed for the very first time. We can't very well go back to the man who first thought of the concept *dog*, but we can trace back rather easily many concepts in many different fields. It's simply a matter of looking them up.

Let's start with the concept *chair*—the concept that proved to be so powerful in Mr. Ames' experiments at Hanover Institute, which I mentioned earlier. Is it possible to go back historically to the first chair? You'll probably be amazed to hear that it is. Of course, chairs were used for kings and noblemen since dimmest antiquity, and ordinary chairs may have been in use for thousands of years in Eastern civilizations. But the chair you are thinking of, the everyday piece of furniture of our Western culture—the movable one-person seat with legs and a back —goes back no farther than Columbus. Up to the end of the fifteenth century the common run of humanity sat uncomfortably on benches and stools. Then, at a definite time and place, Western man arrived at the concept of the chair. Open Mr. Siegfried Giedion's *Mechanization*

Takes Command (a fascinating history of all sorts of things from Yale locks to bathtubs) on page 268 and you will find the boldface heading **The Chair Makes Its Appearance, ca. 1490.** And on the next page you will find a photograph of the ancestor of our chairs: an uncomfortable-looking wooden chair with a narrow, straight slat sticking up in the back. It was part of the original furniture of the famous Strozzi palace in Florence.

Let's stay right there in Florence and trace the origin of another basic concept of Western civilization: the opera. The opera, it turns out, is about a hundred years younger than the chair. The first one on record, called *Dafne,* was written by two Florence musicians, Jacopo Peri and Giulio Caccini, around 1597. The score of that work is lost but we do have the scores of two operas with the same title, *Euridice,* both of which were performed in 1600 for the wedding of Marie de' Medici and Henry IV of France. That time Peri and Caccini worked in competition, composing two different musical settings for the same libretto. Peri's *Euridice* was performed in the spring and Caccini's in December. And that's why the *Oxford History of Music* says of Peri's rather than Caccini's *Euridice* that "it has the singular distinction of forming the actual starting point of modern opera."

Next, let's look at literary history. What was the birthday of the novel? Easy: It's in all the books. The first novel in the modern sense was published in 1678. It was *The Princess of Cleves* by the French author, Madame de La Fayette. As Dunlop's old *History of Prose Fiction* quaintly puts it,

> . . . it may justly be esteemed the earliest of those agreeable and purely fictitious productions, whose province it is to bring about natural events by natural means, and which preserve curiosity alive without the help of wonder—in which human life is exhibited in its true state, diversified only by accidents that daily happen in the world, and influenced only by passions which are actually to be found in our intercourse with mankind.

But maybe you consider novels and operas unimportant compared to the great concepts of science. All right, let's move over into the field of mathematics. Possibly the most important concept the mathematicians claim as their own is the concept of zero, together with the idea of showing values by position. Can the idea of zero be traced back to its historical origin? It certainly can be and has been. Zero was first mentioned in the works of the famous Hindu mathematician, Aryabhatta, around A.D. 500. Later the Hindus passed the idea on to the Arabs, and toward the end of the Middle Ages the Arabs passed it on to Western Europeans.

Or let's look at physics and the concept of gravity. Every schoolboy knows the story about that one: Newton and the apple. The apple, of course, is nothing but a picturesque legend; that particular apple probably never fell off a tree. But there's no question whatever about Newton's working out the modern theory of gravitation. He published it first in 1687 in his book, *Principia Mathematica.*

The social sciences have their basic concepts too. In economics, for instance, there is the concept of a corporation. How old are corporations? Just about four hundred years, say the historians. Corporations go back to the English joint-stock companies, and the first of those was formed in 1553 "for the discovery of the northern parts of the world." The capital of that granddaddy of DuPont and General Motors was £6,000 and the shares were £25 apiece.

Our next exhibit, in the field of political science, is the concept of national sovereignty—surely an essential piece of everybody's mental equipment nowadays. All historians agree that the development of the concept of sovereignty was a one-man affair: the man was the Frenchman Jean Bodin and his book on the subject was published in 1576.

Now let's wander over into sociology. The prize concept of the sociologists is a fascinating one: love. Yes, I know what you're going to say: The idea of finding the origin of the concept *love* is preposterous. But wait a minute. What the sociologists have in mind is "romantic love" in contrast to all other species of love—the love that tends to idealize the beloved, the "fated" kind, the You-were-meant-for-me-and-I-was-meant-for-you type. That idea, historians assure us, hasn't always been around—at least not in our Western culture. It dates back, they tell us, to the days of chivalry, the twelfth-century troubadours, and eventually to the Arabs, who brought the idea to Europe from the East. There is a full analysis of the matter in the book *Love in the Western World* by the Swiss writer Denis de Rougemont, who found the earliest traces of romantic love in the Tristan and Isolde myth. He says flatly: "The earliest passionate lovers whose story has reached us are Abelard and Heloise, who lived in the first half of the twelfth century; and it is in the middle of this same century that love was first recognized and encouraged as a passion worth cultivating."

Surprised? Well, the sociologists have an even more surprising fact to add to the story: according to them, twentieth-century America is the first and only country in history that has made romantic love *the* accepted basis of marriage.

There's another of the great concepts of mankind—*progress*—that also had a whole book devoted to it: *The Idea of Progress* by John Bagnell Bury. Bury defines the idea of progress like this: "Civilization has moved, is moving, and will move in a desirable direction." Do you believe that? Most probably you do. The idea seems firmly rooted in almost every civilized person's mind nowadays. Want to know who thought of it first? Bury says it was the French writer Fontenelle. He went into the matter in 1683 in a book called *Dialogues of the Dead*.

Finally, let's have a look at that important concept of American life—*success*. Not just any kind of success, but the kind that's defined in Webster's dictionary as "the attainment of wealth, position, fame, favor, or the like." In other words, the success-story kind of success. Does this idea, too, have a birthday?

There isn't any convenient place where this information can be found, so I had to do a little research of my own. It seems that the idea of success, in our culture, is a matter connected with religion. No one thought of considering the striving for wealth and position in a favorable light until the churches after the Reformation dropped their original attitude against sinful worldly ambition. It was Martin Luther who first encouraged people to work hard at their "calling." Gradually, according to the sociologists Max Weber and R. H. Tawney, this became the accepted thing and the idea of rising socially through a trade or profession took hold. Tawney, in fact, spotted what seems to be the first "success" or self-improvement book ever written: *The Tradesman's Calling* by Richard Steele. (Not *the* Sir Richard Steele; just a namesake.)

Steele, a retired minister, wrote his book in 1684. If you're curious to know what a seventeenth-century self-help book sounds like, here's a sample:

> Let the religious Tradesman be excited to the practice of industry. It conduces much (under the favour of providence) to our temporal *prosperity*; the diligent are usually blessed with plenty; and no doubt affluence is a blessing, notwithstanding the frequent perversion of it, or else it had never been made the subject of so many divine promises; if riches and honor are good for you, this is the *way* to attain them; for, as there is no calling so great but *sloth will impoverish*, so there are few so mean, but diligence will improve.

Not so very different from today's "how to" books, is it?

And now let's see where we are. Just for the fun of it, let's line up our ten concepts:

Zero	ca. 500
Romantic Love	ca. 1150
Chair	ca. 1490
Corporation	1553
Sovereignty	1576
Opera	1600
Novel	1678
Progress	1683
Success	1684
Gravity	1687

There are a couple of interesting things about this little table. Most of the concepts were born in the sixteenth and seventeenth centuries; in fact, the last four within a period of nine years. This may seem odd to you, but it simply shows that most of our mental furniture was made during or after the Renaissance and Reformation period. Two of the concepts we happened to include were older: *zero* and *romantic love.* Both of them supposedly were imported from Asia by way of the Arabs.

But the most interesting thing about the table is the fact that it can be drawn up at all. You may quarrel with some of the items in it; and you may certainly quarrel with a good many of the dates. But the fact remains that here are ten concepts, taken at random, that can be traced back historically, that had a beginning, that appeared one day for the first time as a nerve cell pattern in someone's brain.

I think if you keep this little table in mind, it will be difficult for you ever to fall into the error that concepts are things. They are not; they are vague references to certain qualities a number of unspecified things have in common.

In other words, they are, by definition, thingummies.

CHAPTER 5

Danger! Language at Work

The individual's whole experience is built upon the plan of his language.
—Henri Delacroix, *Les Grandes Formes de la Vie Mentale*

In the fall of 1786, Goethe went on his famous trip to Italy. Three weeks after he got there, he wrote in his diary:

We northerners can say *Good night!* at any hour of parting in the dark. But the Italian says *Felicissima notte!* only once: at the parting of day and night, when the lamp is brought into the room. To him it means something entirely different. So untranslatable are the idioms of every language: from the highest to the lowest word everything is based on national peculiarities of character, attitudes, or conditions.

Goethe's casual observation contains a profound truth. Every word in every language is part of a system of thinking unlike any other. Speakers of different languages live in different worlds; or rather, they live in the same world, but can't help looking at it in different ways. Words stand for patterns of experience. As one generation hands its language down to the next, it also hands down a fixed pattern of thinking, seeing, and feeling. When we go from one language to another, nothing stays put; different peoples carry different nerve patterns in their brains, and there's no point where they fully match.

Of course, Goethe wasn't the only one who noticed this. Everybody who comes in contact with foreign languages sooner or later runs into the same thing. In recent years, UN meetings have furnished many examples. When the UN charter was written, Latin-Americans protested that the phrase *sovereign equality* didn't mean a thing to them; they preferred *personality of states*, a phrase meaningless to everyone else. The French, it turned out, had no word for *trusteeship*, the Chinese had trouble in translating *steering committee*, the Spanish-speaking members couldn't express the difference between *chairman* and *president*. The Russians had trouble with *gentlemen's agreement* and had to fall back on semi-English, making it *gentlemenskoye soglasheniye*.

Russian is filled with words showing the Russian "character, attitudes and conditions." The critic Edmund Wilson found that out when he read Tolstoy in the original. He came upon such beauties as *dozhidat'sya* (to attain by waiting), *propivat'sya* (to squander all one's money on drink), and *pereparyvat'* (to whip everybody all around). And in *Anna Karenina* he found no fewer than fifteen words that meant different expressions of the eyes.

The more exotic the language, the odder the thinking pattern to us. In Hindustani the same word, *kal*, stands for yesterday and tomorrow. In Lithuanian there is a word for gray when you speak of eyes, another when you speak of hair, a third when you speak of ducks and geese, several more for other purposes, but no word for gray in general. In Balinese there is a lovely word, *tis*, that means "to feel warm when it's cold or cool when it's hot."

We don't even have to go that far to realize differences in language patterns. They are brought home to every first-year French student when he is asked to translate a simple sentence like "The girl is running down the stairs." Naturally, he tries to translate word for word: *"La petite fille court bas l'escalier."* Then he learns that that's all wrong. A Frenchman says: *"La petite fille descend l'escalier en courant"*—the girl descends the stairs in running.

Or take German. Everybody has heard of the three German genders, which make tables, chairs, coats and spoons masculine, cats, roads, bridges and forks feminine, and horses, sheep, girls and knives neuter. Or the two German forms of *you*—familiar *Du* and formal *Sie*—whose subtle difference may spell the loss of a job or the acceptance of a marriage proposal.

German has all sorts of fine distinctions that don't exist in English. A German isn't satisfied with a word meaning "to know"; he needs two, *wissen* and *kennen*. One means "to have knowledge of," as in knowing a secret; the other means "to be acquainted with," as in knowing a place or a person. A German woman doesn't just "put on" a dress, an apron, or a hat; she "pulls a dress on," "ties an apron around," and "puts a hat on top of herself." A German horse has a different name depending on whether it's white or black: if it's white, it's a *Schimmel*; if it's black, it's a *Rappe*.

Even more subtly, German writers come in two grades. They may be either *Schriftsteller* (professionals who make a living by writing) or *Dichter* (poets in verse or prose; literary figures). Thomas Mann is a *Dichter*, but Vicki Baum is a *Schriftstellerin*. In German translation, Ernest Hemingway doubtless is a *Dichter*, but Erle Stanley Gardner is a *Schriftsteller*.

To a German, of course, some of our English distinctions are just as odd. *Braten*, in German, covers roasting, baking, grilling, broiling and frying; *Reise* means travel, journey, voyage, cruise, tour and trip. So don't get me wrong—don't consider the English language pattern natural and all others perverse. It all depends on where you sit.

Just for the fun of it, I drew up a short list of German "untranslatables" (with explanations in English of what they mean almost but not quite). Here they are:

Lebenskünstler	one who knows how to live
Sehnsucht	great longing or yearning
Zeitgeist	spirit of the age
Weltschmerz	world-weariness
Rausch	drunkenness, delirium, passionate glow, ecstasy, mad fit
verscherzen	to lose something through folly, to trifle away
Gemütlichkeit	good-natured, sanguine, easy-going disposition; good nature; cheerfulness; comfortableness; sentiment; freedom from worry about money
Schadenfreude	malicious joy at another's misfortune; gratification of pent-up envy; joy over the misfortune of those one has formerly cringed to and envied
Übermut	wild spirits; excessive joy or merriment; cockiness; sauciness; uppishness; arrogance

Naturally, English has its share of "untranslatables" too. They don't seem any different from other words to us, but foreigners have an awful time with them. Examples: "to humor someone," "a bargain," "a pet."

On the other hand, there are quite a few useful words that other languages have but we have not. We have no single word that means "his or her" and have to make shift with sentences like "Everybody put on their hats and coats." We have no word for "brother or sister" and our sociologists had to invent the word *sibling* for the purpose. We have no short way of saying that one thing makes another one possible, unless we misuse the word *enable* and say "The new bridge enabled a speed-up in traffic."

And, as John T. Winterich noted in the *Saturday Review of Literature* a while ago, we have no noun "to denote the relationship of one father-in-law (or mother-in-law) to his (or her) opposite number." You may doubt—looking at the world through your own culture-and-language spectacles—whether any people ever went to the trouble of coining a word for such a complex relationship. But you'd be mistaken. As soon as national "peculiarities of character, attitudes or conditions" make a relationship important and meaningful, a label for it will appear. Yiddish, for one, is a language equipped with Mr. Winterich's word: the mutual father-in-law is a *mekhoótn*, the mutual mother-in-law a *mekhtáynesta*.

Words for family relationships, in fact, are the pet examples of the anthropologists to show cultural differences among languages. The variations are endless. To you, an uncle is an uncle; to millions of people there is a tremendous difference between a father's brother and a mother's brother. In English, the word *cousin* covers both girls and boys; in practically all other languages, such an idea would be utterly unthinkable.

Consider, for instance, the fantastically complex system of the Vietnamese. They wouldn't think of using the term for the father's elder brother, *bac*, for the father's younger brother, who is called *chu*, not to speak of the mother's brother, who is called *cau*. The father's sister is *co*; the mother's sister is *di*. On the other hand, one word, *chau*, is all they use to refer to grandchildren, great-grandchildren, nephews, nieces, grandnephews, grandnieces and so on of either sex. A son, when he grows up, is suddenly called *cau*, like the mother's brother; so is a wife's brother after he gets married. Before that, he is called *anh*, "elder brother," which is also the term used by a wife for her husband's elder brother, as well as for her husband himself. If this sounds utterly confusing to you, please remember that our system is probably just as confusing to the Vietnamese.

Anthropologists soon learn not to be bewildered by varieties of words. The Eskimos have one word for "snow on the ground," another for "falling snow," a third for "drifting snow" and a fourth for "a snow-drift." They have a general word for "seal," another for "seal basking in the sun," a third for "seal floating on a piece of ice," and any number of others classifying seals by age and sex. To the Chukchee, a tribe that lives at the far eastern tip of Siberia, reindeer are what seals are to the Eskimos. They have twenty-six different words for reindeer skin colors, and sixteen words for reindeer of various ages and sexes. For instance, a *qlikin*, a male baby reindeer, is different from a *penvel*, a male reindeer one to two years old; a *krimqor* (female, two to three years old) is not the same as a *rewkut* (female, five to six years old); and so on through sixteen different names—a system which comes perfectly naturally to even the dumbest Chukchee boys and girls. Halfway around the globe, the Lapps of northern Scandinavia also live of, by and for reindeer. *They* call them *patso, sarves, hierke, svaljes, vateuvaja, stainak, ratno, tjnoivak, kiepak, pajuk* or *tjousek*, depending on sex, color, fertility, tractability and whatnot. Of course their classification has nothing to do with the Chukchee system; no reason why it should.

If you feel superior to all this and insist that a reindeer is a reindeer (except for specially famous ones like Donder, Blitzen or Rudolph), that just shows you don't realize the close relation between language and life. For Lapps or Chukchees, a single word for reindeer would be the height of inconvenience; they *have* to make all these distinctions to get on with the business of living. To them, the sentence "I saw a reindeer" would be as absurd as if *you* said: "I live in a dwelling with family members and own a vehicle."

Anthropologists also often run into a single word used by a primitive tribe that seems almost impossible to define exactly. One of them once spent fourteen months in the Solomon Islands, using most of that time trying to pin down the meaning of the word *mumi* in a Papuan dialect. It was easy to see that a *mumi* was a chief headman, wealthy, a born leader, and owned a clubhouse filled with wooden gongs, which was used ever so often for big parties. But it took much research to find some of the other connotations of the word *mumi*:

> He is given preference over other natives in pig-buying; the choicest cuts of pork go to him; he need never climb palms for drinking nuts if someone else is around. . . . He can sit in his clubhouse and listen to the flattery of his followers, he can call upon supernatural aid whenever he needs it, and he can rest assured of a comfortable place in the afterworld.

Quite a word, isn't it?

All of these examples, however, are nothing compared to the brilliant researches of our own anthropologists into the structure of American Indian languages. Fortunately for the science of linguistics, the Indians live right among us, while their languages are as far removed from ours as they can possibly be. They are full of eye-opening examples of the enormous range and flexibility of the human mind. Better than anything else, they show that the very nature of facts and events changes as soon as another language is used to state them.

Here are some of our anthropologists' findings:

In the Kwakiutl language, there is no single word that means "to sit." There are only words that mean "sitting on the ground," "sitting on the beach," "sitting on a pile of things," "sitting on a round thing," or "sitting on the floor of the house."

In Dakota, there is one word meaning "to be gripped" that covers a wide range of situations that seem utterly different to us. Depending on the context it may mean "to kick," "to tie in bundles," "to bite," "to be near to," "to pound" and so on.

Dakota verbs are equipped to express subtle degrees. *Slecha,* for example, means "to split something easily"; *shlecha* means "to split something with some difficulty"; *hlecha* means "to split something with great difficulty." *Zezeya* means "dangling"; but *apazhezheya* means "right on the edge, almost falling over."

In Hupa, nouns have present, past and future tenses. *Xonta* means "house now," *xontaneen* means "house past (in ruins)," *xontate* means "house to be (planned)."

The Shawnee translation of the English sentence "I pull the branch aside" is *nilthawakona.* Broken down into its elements, this means "Fork tree by-hand I do." The Shawnee translation of "I clean it (a gun) with a ramrod" is *nipekwalakha*—which means "I dry-space inside-hole by-moving-tool do."

In Nootka, there are no parts of speech whatever. The difference between nouns and verbs, or between subjects and predicates, simply doesn't exist. There is a word for "house," for instance, but it's something indefinite between a noun and a verb and means "it houses." Or take the simple English sentence, "He invites people to a feast." In our language, this has a subject ("he"), a verb ("invites") and a neat logical progression—that is, according to *our* logic, the way of thinking embodied in our language. A Nootka Indian looks at this situation in an entirely different way. He starts *his* sentence with the main thing about a feast—the event of boiling or cooking: *tlimsh*. Then comes *ya*, meaning "result": *tlimshya*, "cooked food." Next comes *is*, "eating," which makes *tlimshya-is*, "eating cooked food." Next: *ita*, "those who do." Now he has *tlimshya-isita*, "cooked food eaters." Finally he adds *itl* ("go for") and *ma* ("he") and comes up with the sentence *tlimshya-isita-itlma*, "cooked food eaters he go for" or, in English, "he invites people to a feast."

And then there is the most fascinating of all Indian languages, Hopi. By now you won't be surprised when I tell you that a Hopi classifies things differently from us. For water he has two words: *pahe* and *keyi*. *Pahe* is a lot of water running wild, so to speak—the sea, a lake, a waterfall; *keyi* is "tamed" water, water in a container—a panful or a glassful. The word *masaytaka* takes in everything that flies except birds. It doesn't bother a Hopi that *masaytaka* may at different times mean an airplane, a pilot, a butterfly, or a mosquito.

Hopi verbs don't have present, past or future tenses; it is a "timeless" language. Instead, its verbs have forms that show whether something is (or was) *actually* happening, whether it is *expected* to happen, or whether it is merely apt to happen *in general*. When a Hopi says *wari* ("running"), it may mean "he is running, I see him"; but it may also mean "he was running, you and I both saw him." When he says *warikni*, it means "I expect him to run," which isn't quite the same as "he will run." And when he says *warikngwe*, it means "he runs" (in general, say, on the track team).

A unique feature of Hopi is that verbs can express one big action or a series of little ones. A suffix ending in *ta* takes care of that. *Yoko* means "he gives one nod"; *yokokota* means "he is nodding." *Ripi* means "it gives one flash"; *ripipita*, "it is sparkling." *Wukuku* means "he takes one step without moving from his place"; *wukukuta*, "he is dancing up and down." *Hochi* means "it forms a sharp angle"; *hochichita*, "it is zigzag."

All of this is as odd as can be, but again I must remind you that it seems odd only to us who are used to thinking in English. Hopi and English are just two of thousands of languages actually spoken today. Each of them, as the late Edward Sapir put it, is a particular *how* of thought; and the speakers of each consider all others as more or less inferior, absurd and illogical.

The knowledge of this basic fact is essential to clear thinking. To be sure, we can't help using our native (or adopted) language in our thoughts; but we can try to remember that ours isn't the only way to think.

Does this mean that the practice of translation will help you think? Maybe it does. Let's go into that question in the next chapter.

CHAPTER 6

The Pursuit of Translation

Translation is at best an echo.

—George Borrow

A few months ago I wrote a *Reader's Digest* article that was translated into German and Spanish. One of the expressions I used was "fancy words." It turned out that you can neither say that in German nor in Spanish. In German the phrase becomes *geschraubte Ausdrücke* ("screwed-up expressions"); in Spanish, *palabras rebuscadas* ("far-fetched words").

What surprised me even more was that the common word *executive* has no counterpart in either German or Spanish. In German it's *leitende Männer* ("leading men"), in Spanish *directores de empresas* ("directors of enterprises").

These are, after all, simple words. Quite another problem came up when Billy Rose's *Wine, Women and Words* had to be translated for the French *Reader's Digest* edition. Maurice Chevalier was hired to do the job and did himself proud—considering what he was up against. He translated "it was a seven-day wonder" into *époustoufla* ("it blew them over"), "it was a cinch bet" into *c'était du nougat!* ("it was candy"), and "razzle-dazzle and razzmatazz" into *plaisanter sur des plaisantries plaisantes* ("having fun with fun").

Translation problems of this sort are not exceptional. Do you think translating means taking the dictionary translations of each word and putting them together? This is a widespread notion; it's the theory of automatic translation. And I mean automatic: in California there is a machine, the Bureau of Standards Western Automatic Computer, that's supposed to translate on just that principle. I haven't seen any of its translations, but I am skeptical. Equivalent words in two languages are not the rule, but the exception.

Recently Monsignor Ronald Knox wrote a little book about Bible translation problems. Among his illustrations are such apparently simple cases as the English word *danger*. Surprisingly enough, it doesn't occur once in the Authorized Version of the Old Testament. Now, says Knox, "it is nonsense to suppose that the Hebrew mind has no such notion as danger; why is there no word for it? The answer can only be, that in Hebrew you express the same idea by a nearly-allied word which has to do duty, also, for slightly different ideas; a word like 'affliction,' 'tribulation' or 'trouble.'" Or take the word *land*: "Neither Hebrew nor Greek nor Latin has two separate words for 'earth,' in the sense of the terrestrial globe, and 'land' in the sense of a particular region of it. When we are told that there was darkness all over the *terra* at the time of our Lord's Crucifixion, how are we to know whether that darkness was world-wide, or was only noticeable in Palestine?"

Then there is the simple word *know*, which, according to Knox, "is a constant problem to the translator, all through the New Testament. Nine times out of ten you want to translate it 'realize' but unfortunately that use of the word 'realize' is modern slang." Even more basically, "Hebrew has one word that does duty for 'and' and 'but'; and wherever the translator comes across that word in the Old Testament he must decide between them, sometimes at the risk of making nonsense of a whole paragraph."

On top of all that, translation, like woman's work, is never done. It has to be done all over again for each succeeding generation. How many English translations of the Bible there are by now, I don't know; but there are over thirty translations of Homer's *Odyssey*, for instance. You'll immediately understand why when you compare different versions of the same passage.

In the standard translation by Butcher and Lang (1879) the famous scene in which Odysseus is recognized by his old dog looks like this:

Thus they spake one to the other. And lo, a hound raised up his head and pricked his ears, even where he lay, Argos, the hound of Odysseus, of the hardy heart, which of old himself had bred, but had got no joy of him, for ere that, he went to sacred Ilios. Now in time past the young men used to lead the hound against wild goats and deer and hares; but as then, despised he lay (his master being afar) in the deep dung of mules and kine, whereof an ample bed was spread before the doors, till the thralls of Odysseus should carry it away to dung therewith his wide demesne. There lay the dog Argos, full of vermin. Yet even now when he was ware of Odysseus standing by, he wagged his tail and dropped both his ears, but nearer to his master he had not now the strength to draw.

Now let's go back to 1725, to the most famous English translation of the *Odyssey*, by Alexander Pope:

> Thus, near the gates conferring as they drew,
> Argus, the dog, his ancient master knew:
> He not unconscious of the voice and tread,
> Lifts to the sound his ear, and rears his head;
> Bred by Ulysses, nourish'd at his board,
> But, ah! not fated long to please his lord;
> To him, his sweetness and his strength were vain;
> The voice of glory call'd him o'er the main.
> Till then in every sylvan chase renown'd,
> With Argus, Argus, rung the woods around;
> With him the youth pursued the goat or fawn,
> Or traced the mazy leveret o'er the lawn.
> Now left to man's ingratitude he lay,
> Unhoused, neglected, in the public way;
> And where on heaps the rich manure was spread,
> Obscene with reptiles, took his sordid bed.
>   He knew his lord; he knew and strove to meet:
> In vain he strove to crawl and kiss his feet;
> Yet (all he could) his tail, his ears, his eyes,
> Salute his master, and confess his joys.

T. E. Lawrence (Lawrence of Arabia) translated the *Odyssey* in 1932. His version is this:

As they talked, a dog lying there lifted his head and pricked his ears. This was Argos whom Odysseus had bred but never worked, because he left for Ilium too soon. On a time the young fellows used to take him out to course the wild goats, the deer, the hares: but now he lay derelict and masterless on the dung-heap before the gates, on the deep bed of mule-droppings and cow-dung which collected there till the serfs of Odysseus had time to carry it off for manuring his broad acres. So lay Argos the hound, all shivering with dog-ticks. Yet the instant Odysseus approached the beast knew him. He thumped his tail and drooped his ears forward, but lacked power to drag himself ever so little towards his master.

You probably feel that the third version is the best. So do I. But all such judgments are relative. When Pope's translation was published, a contemporary critic wrote: "To say of this noble work that it is the best which ever appeared of the kind, would be speaking in much lower terms than it deserves." Sixty years later, in 1788, William Cowper said flatly: "There is hardly a thing in the world of which Pope is so entirely destitute as a taste for Homer." As to T. E. Lawrence, Professor Gilbert Highet of Columbia University casually remarked in a book review the other day: "T. E. Lawrence's caricature of Homer's *Odyssey* is clever but cheap, like a mock-Victorian drawing-room."

Another paradox of translation is this: The simpler the words of the original, the harder it is to translate them. That's why simple lyrics are the toughest translation problem in the world. Compare, for instance, four English translations of Goethe's *Wanderers Nachtlied*, which is generally considered *the* most beautiful German poem. Here is the original—all twenty-four words of it:

> Über allen Gipfeln
> Ist Ruh,
> In allen Wipfeln
> Spürest du
> Kaum einen Hauch;
> Die Vögelein schweigen im Walde.
> Warte nur, balde
> Ruhest du auch.

Here is Longfellow:

> O'er all the hill-tops
> Is quiet now,
> In all the tree-tops
> Hearest thou
> Hardly a breath;
> The birds are asleep in the trees:
> Wait; soon like these
> Thou too shalt rest.

Aytoun and Martin:

> Peace breathes along the shade
> Of every hill,
> The tree-tops of the glade
> Are hush'd and still;
> All woodland murmurs cease,
> The birds to rest within the brake are gone.
> Be patient, weary heart—anon,
> Thou too, shalt be at peace!

George Sylvester Viereck:

> Over the tops of the trees
> Night reigns. No breath, no breeze.
> Never a voice is heard
> Of rustling leaf or bird
>   The forest through.
> Hush! But a little ways
> From where your footstep strays
>   Peace awaits you.

John Rothensteiner:

> Over all the hill tops
>   Is peace;
> In all the trees' still tops
>   Gently cease
> The breaths from the blue.
> The birds in the forest are sleeping,
>   Soon in God's keeping
> Sleepest thou too.

Which is best? The one that's printed in all the anthologies is Long-fellow's, of course; the one that's nearest to the letter and spirit of the original, I think, is Rothensteiner's. But it doesn't really matter: none of the four comes anywhere close to the original with its magically soft and soothing German words.

If you don't know German, I can't very well ask you to appreciate that. In fact, it seems almost impossible to talk understandably about translation to a person who may not know any foreign language. There-fore, I want to add here one more example, this time the other way round: I'll show you an English passage and describe the various words that have been used to translate it into German. (I apologize for draw-ing so much on my native language.) My example are the famous lines from *Macbeth*:

> Out, out, brief candle!
> Life's but a walking shadow, a poor player
> That struts and frets his hour upon the stage
> And then is heard no more: it is a tale
> Told by an idiot, full of sound and fury,
> Signifying nothing.

The Germans have about as many Shakespeare translations as we have Homer translations. I compared eight different versions of this passage and found eight different expressions for "struts and frets," five for "idiot," and six for "sound and fury." For "struts and frets" a German reader gets something like: makes a noise and raves, swaggers and gnashes, labors and raves, stilts and gnashes, parades and raves, rages and storms, stilts and brags, and boasts; for "idiot": blockhead, fool, madman, simpleton and ninny; for "sound and fury": pomposity, noise and rage, flood of words, storm and urge, tone and fire.

Reading this, you probably sympathize with the poor Germans who get only a vague inkling of Shakespeare's immortal words. But remember that most of these translations are excellent: one is by Schiller, one is by the famous team of Schlegel and Tieck, and so on. On the whole, they are just as good as *our* translations of Goethe—or of Homer, Plato, Horace, Dante, Cervantes, Balzac, Tolstoy and all the rest. You just have to accept the fact that translations are always approximations; as Don Quixote said, they show us the wrong side of the tapestry.

But even that isn't all. Often a complete shift is necessary in order to convey anything at all in another language. Two recent Broadway plays furnish good examples.

In his translation of Jean Giraudoux's *Madwoman of Chaillot*, Maurice Valency completely changed a great many passages that meant a lot to Frenchmen but would have left Americans cold. For instance, a character, in the role of a billionaire, says: "I have flowers sent from Java, where they are cut from the backs of elephants, and if the petals are the least bit crushed, I fire the elephant-drivers." In English he says instead: "I dispatch a plane to Java for a bouquet of flowers. I send a steamer to Egypt for a basket of figs. I send a special representative to New York to fetch an ice cream cone, and if it's not exactly right, back it goes."

And when Arthur Miller's famous play *Death of a Salesman* was produced in Vienna, the leading part, believe it or not, was played as a sort of petty official. Otherwise the Viennese wouldn't have understood what it was all about.

What does all this mean to *you*? It means that translating is the ideal form of intellectual exercise. Whenever we translate, we are forced to abandon the mental patterns we are used to and get the hang of others completely alien to our thinking. There's nothing quite like it to gain mental flexibility—which, as you'll see later on, is practically *the* main ingredient of clear thinking. If foreign languages didn't exist, we'd have to invent them as a training device for our minds.

This looks like a plug for the study of foreign languages, but I don't quite mean that—at least not in the usual sense. Usually foreign languages are played up either because they are practical ("You ought to know how to order a meal in Paris") or because they are cultural ("Latin makes you think more logically"). The way I look at it, all that's neither here nor there. Let Schopenhauer make my point for me:

In learning any foreign language, you form new concepts, you discover relationships you didn't realize before, innumerable nuances, similarities, differences enter your mind; you get a rounded view of everything. Which means that you think differently in every language, that learning a language modifies and colors your thinking, corrects and improves your views, and increases your thinking skill, *since it will more and more detach your ideas from your words.*

Schopenhauer, who was an intellectual snob, goes on to say that everybody ought to know Latin and Greek—in fact, that people who don't are only half-human. I don't think that follows from his argument. If language study is good because it detaches ideas from words, any language will do—Chinese, Swahili, Navaho—the farther removed from our own culture the better. To be sure, some languages have richer literatures than others, but that's another story.

Probably you'll be skeptical about all this; interest in foreign languages doesn't come naturally to an American. But before you shrug it off, let me remind you that ever since the Romans, Western civilization was built and run by people who knew at least one foreign language; that until not so long ago, Latin and Greek were part of every educated person's mental equipment. As the famous quotation goes, the battle of Waterloo was won on the playing fields of Eton; it's equally true that the British Empire was won in the *classrooms* of Eton, where future colonial administrators were forced to compose little Latin poems.

Well, then, do you have to go to a Berlitz school to learn the art of clear thinking? Not quite. As I said, the important thing is not the learning of foreign languages, but the activity of translation. Fortunately, you can practice translation—to a degree—even if you don't know a single foreign word. You can translate from English into English. You do this whenever you detach ideas from one set of words and attach them to another. You do it whenever you write a letter and make your ideas clear to the addressee; whenever you make a speech and present your thoughts to your audience; whenever you carry on an intelligent conversation. You can learn to do this sort of translating better and better, and you can use it consciously "to detach your ideas from your words."

Otherwise you never can tell whether you *have* any ideas—or just words.

CHAPTER 7

First Aid for Word Trouble

I am not so lost in lexicography as to forget that words are the daughters of earth, and that things are the sons of heaven.

—Samuel Johnson, Preface to his *Dictionary*

Getting impatient? I'm afraid you are. Here you are, starting the seventh chapter of a book on clear thinking, and still there's nothing you can put your finger on—no practical stuff, no rules, no formulas. You have read about lobotomies, and mental imagery, and Indian languages; but will all that help you improve your thinking?

Before you say no, let me put down a short list of the points we've covered so far.

1. All thinking is the manipulation of memories. Even "inspirations" are based on your experience and nothing else.

2. Your memories are patterns of nerve cells in your brain. When you remember, you activate these patterns electrically.

3. All memories are more or less distorted. Your brain registers experience differently from everybody else's.

4. Abstract ideas are the patterns two or more memories have in common. They are born whenever someone realizes that similarity.

5. Translation helps your thinking because you use two sets of nerve patterns instead of one. This includes translation into other English words.

All this is far from useless information. In fact, if you were able to remember these five points constantly during all your waking and thinking hours, you could stop reading right now and say you have mastered

The Library
Saint Francis College
Fort Wayne 1.

the art of clear thinking. You could even go further and boil the five points down to two:

1. Don't forget that everybody, including yourself, has only his own experience to think with.

2. Detach your ideas from your words.

As long as you keep these two points in mind, you are a top-notch clear thinker and your problem is solved.

The trouble is, of course, that nobody can do that. Life goes so fast, and we have to think about so much, that we can't at any given moment remember how our brain is organized, and how everybody else's brain is organized, and how the English language is organized. We have to do our thinking as we go along, acting *as if* words were ideas and *as if* ideas were the same in everybody's mind. The best we can do is remember the true facts about thinking from time to time, and use short cuts and rules-of-thumb to deal with everyday problems.

And that's what you'll find in the rest of this book.

The first short cut I have to offer deals with abstractness and concreteness. Obviously, not all words and ideas are on the same level of thinking: some are fairly concrete (like the concept *chair*), some are rather abstract (like the concept of a *novel*). Some are completely abstract and general (like "the good, the true and the beautiful"), some are as concrete and specific as possible (like "this book, which you are now holding in your hand"). As you see, there is a sliding scale here; it's a question of degree. That's what makes it hard to orient yourself quickly and know, while you are thinking or listening or reading, just what level you are on at the moment. If you could do that, it would make clear thinking easier for you; you could tell whether you are deep in words or close to things.

Naturally, there wouldn't be any problem if abstract and concrete concepts were always black and white. There's no trouble in telling them apart when you see them one right next to the other with a sharp contrast between them.

I had a wonderful time hunting up some examples to show you this black-and-white effect. I found that when you suddenly plunge from the abstract into the concrete, or from the concrete into the abstract, you'll invariably get something funny. In fact, I made a little discovery: I got a new slant on the difference between wit and humor. When you go from the abstract to the concrete, you get humor: you particularize, you turn to people, things, characters, situations. When you go from the concrete to the abstract, you get wit: you generalize, you turn to words and ideas.

For example, let's take a great humorist and watch his trick of turning from the abstract to the concrete. Here are some of the famous "Wellerisms" from Dickens' *Pickwick Papers*:

"Business first, pleasure arterwards, as King Richard the Third said when he stabbed t'other king in the Tower, afore he smothered the babbies."

"It's over, and can't be helped, and that's one consolation, as they always says in Turkey, ven they cuts the wrong man's head off."

"I only assisted natur', ma'am, as the doctor said to the boy's mother, arter he'd bled him to death."

"That's what I call a self-evident proposition, as the dog's-meat man said, when the housemaid told him he warn't a gentleman."

"Vich I call addin' insult to injury, as the parrot said ven they not only took him from his native land, but made him talk the English langwidge arterwards."

In contrast, let's see how a writer gets witty effects by going from the specific and concrete to the general and abstract. One of my favorite humorists, P. G. Wodehouse, has a trick of deriving general rules from extremely special situations. Here are some of these "Wodehouse maxims":

"The attitude of fellows toward finding girls in their bedroom shortly after midnight varies."

"It's always embarrassing to run unexpectedly into a girl you used to be engaged to."

"A visitor at a country house with something to hide is a good deal restricted in choice of caches."

"Bedridden ladies of advanced age seldom bubble over with fun and joie de vivre."

After all these examples I am sure you'll know what I mean by abstract and concrete. But, as I said, the problem is not the black-and-white type of thing, but different shades of gray. If we want a handy guide, we have to find a way of drawing a line.

Now here is my short-cut method of doing this. Let's arbitrarily call one kind of words "abstract" and another kind "concrete" and see whether the thought is expressed in one kind or the other. Assign a label to each word this way. (What follows is a simplified version of a rather complicated statistical formula I worked out. If you're interested in the more exact method, you'll find it in the Appendix on pages 183-188.)

Our "concrete" words are those whose meaning is fixed whatever language you use. They are:

1. Names of people.
2. Numbers and number words.
3. Dates, etc. (Clock and calendar words.)
4. Words that are male or female. ("Natural gender," the grammarians call it.)
5. Words that point to one specific person. (I, you, he, she, my, your, his, her.)

In addition, let's call "concrete" all words made more specific by a word in one of these five groups. For instance, the word *ideas*, standing by itself, is obviously an "abstract" word; but we'll label it "concrete" when it appears as *Joe's ideas, two ideas, last year's ideas, a woman's ideas, your ideas.*

And that ends the list of "concrete" words in our scheme; all others are "abstract." Now we can go ahead and estimate concreteness or abstractness in a jiffy. All we have to do is mark "concrete" words and see how they stack up against the others.

Let's practice on an easy example. The other day, my eye fell on a newspaper advertisement—or rather, it was drawn strongly by the picture of a girl in a French bathing suit and the headline ADVICE TO WOMEN ONLY. The ad started as follows: "If you want a more slender looking figure—do as many famous movie stars do. Use passive exercise."

If you analyze these words with the little yardstick I've given you, you'll find that the only "concrete" word here is *you*. All others are "abstract," particularly the mysterious expression *passive exercise*. In other words, the thought expressed here is on a high level of abstraction and if you want to get at a specific meaning, you need a translation onto a lower language level. *Passive exercise* by itself isn't a meaningful expression; rather, it is an interesting combination of words that whets your appetite for more specific language.

Which is, of course, exactly what the proponents of *passive exercise* had in mind. Further down in the ad, they said: "Telephone and we will give you all information without embarrassment or obligation."

Now let's take some very concrete language. Forgetting about the reasons for *passive exercise*, let's recklessly look up the recipe for twenty-minute fudge in Fannie Farmer's cookbook:

1 egg, well beaten	4 squares chocolate, melted with
3 tablespoons cream	1 tablespoon butter
1 teaspoon vanilla	1 cup chopped walnut meats or
¼ teaspoon salt	marshmallows cut in pieces, or
1 pound confectioners' sugar	half each

Mix ingredients in order given. Spread in buttered pan, 8 x 8 inches. Cool and cut in squares. Makes 1½ pounds.

I don't need to tell you that practically all the words here are "concrete"—numbers, or words specified by numbers and measures. (See Point 2 on the list on page 54.) No need to telephone Fannie Farmer for an explanation of what all this means in practical terms. It's all here. If you count, you'll find it's about 60 per cent concrete—about as concrete as the English language can get.

Next, after these two practice runs, let's see how the method works in analyzing advertising or propaganda. To kill two birds with one stone, I have chosen something halfway between advertising and propaganda—two institutional advertisements dealing with the theme of free enterprise. To make the "concrete" words easy to spot, I have put them in italics. Here is Exhibit A:

(Picture of an eagle)

FREEDOM IS A TOUGH OLD BIRD

You've heard it said that we must protect our freedom lest it be lost.

The reverse is even truer. Why not let our freedoms protect us, lest we be lost?

For freedom isn't delicate—it's a tough, old bird. Freedom has always been, and is *today*, the source of America's strength.

Our freedom to think, to choose, to act has not only enriched the American character—it has given us a material standard of living that is the envy of the world.

We are able to take for granted television and autos, food and clothing in abundance, precisely because freedom emancipates the mind and hand. Freedom is constructive—while tyranny confines *man* and finally destroys *him.*

That is why, in time to come, the best protection of our freedom will be more freedom.

It will enable America to resist tyranny without resorting to it . . . to form a great military force without being militarized . . . to save a world without enslaving it.

In this climate of freedom, Burlington Mills will continue to do what it could do nowhere else on earth: fulfill the responsibility of its freedom by creating better fabrics, at better prices, for more people.

Burlington Mills

Next, Exhibit B:

(Picture of a tool chest marked "W. P. Chrysler")

THE TOOLS THAT MONEY COULDN'T BUY

Walter Chrysler made them *himself.* That is *his* original *tool chest* too. *He* was *17,* working in a railroad roundhouse. *His* mechanic's *fingers* itched for a kit of tools of *his own.* So young *Walter* got steel and made *his own.*

As *he* shaped and turned and tempered them, *he* shaped a dream as well. It was a special American kind of dream—free-ranging imagination anchored to solid things like common sense, and working a little harder, and making things a little better. And asking no odds of anyone.

It led *Walter Chrysler* to success in railroading when *he* was still young. It led *him* to study the automobiles other *men* were beginning to make. Why couldn't a *man* build better cars than any known—nimbler, safer, more comfortable, handsomer?

So, *25 years ago, Walter Chrysler* introduced the *first* Chrysler *car.* What *he* did changed the whole pattern of American motoring. *He* changed it with high-compression engines, *4-wheel* hydraulic brakes, all-steel bodies, new ways of distributing weight for better riding . . . and all the many originations the entire automobile industry eventually followed.

As Chrysler Corporation *this year* observes its *25th anniversary,* it seems a fitting thing to recall this significant event in recent contemporary history—to pay this tribute to *Walter Chrysler* and *his* creative *genius.*

And the tools of *his* earlier mechanic's *days? I* remember when *he* found them in *his mother's* house. It was long after *I* had come to know *him,* long after *he* had asked *me* to work with *him. He* brought the tools back from Kansas. A few of them needed fixing and *he* asked *me* to fix them. It was a compliment *I* have never forgotten.

The qualities *Mr. Chrysler* put into *his own tools he* also wrought into the great organization that bears *his* name. *He* built not merely material things; *he* inspired *men* with a zeal to carry on the splendid ideals *he* had set for them.

Chrysler Corporation is still young enough to feel and be guided by the inspiration of its founder. *He* wished this company always to be a producer of fine automobiles of great value.

And those of us who were privileged to work with *him* believe that the new Plymouth, Dodge, DeSoto and Chrysler automobiles live up to *his tradition.*

It is a tradition uniquely American—to live and work with the idea of finding better ways to make what people want.

K. T. *Keller*
President, Chrysler Corporation

You can see at a glance that the Burlington Mills ad has practically no "concrete" words—just *today* (a calendar word), *man* (a male word), *you, him.* Otherwise it's all high-level language, abstract, general, metaphorical. The Chrysler ad, however, is well sprinkled with "concrete" words. Not as many as the fudge recipe, to be sure—about 20 per cent—but enough to make the argument factual and down-to-earth.

Does this mean that Burlington Mills' argument is wrong, and Chrysler's right? Not necessarily. In fact, both ads say essentially the same thing—that the free enterprise system is good. But if you want to argue the point, there's nothing to argue with in the Burlington Mills ad: it's all words. On the other hand, Walter Chrysler's tool chest is a square, hard fact. It's something to think about, while the tough old bird freedom is something you might as well skip.

So, if it is a piece of writing you have to think about, try to orient yourself first and find out what level it is on. If it's concrete, well and good; if it's highly abstract, it may not be worth bothering with. Look again at the five points on page 54. Does the writing mention names, dates, numbers, people? How often? Take a pencil and underline the "concrete" words. What do you have? A page well filled with penciled lines? Or just a little island of concreteness here and there?

After you've done this a few times, you'll jump from one concrete island to the next, like Eliza crossing the ice, refusing to be drowned in the abstract words. Try it on an editorial in your newspaper. Or, for that matter, try it on the next speech you are called upon to make; it may help you keep your audience awake. (If you want to go further, try the more exact method described in the appendix; it's harder to do, but more instructive.)

Of course, all this doesn't mean that abstractions should always be disregarded. On the contrary, abstract concepts are powerful tools for thinking—*as long as they are backed up by references to people, things and events.* But abstractions all by themselves—that's another story. If you want one more example, here is a paragraph that appeared in the first issue of *The Freeman,* a newly founded conservative magazine:

In terms of current labels, The Freeman will be at once radical, liberal, conservative and reactionary. It will be radical because it will go to the root of questions. It will be liberal because it will stand for the maximum of individual liberty, for tolerance of all honest diversity of opinion, and for faith in the efficacy of solving our internal problems by discussion and reason rather than suppression and force. It will be conservative because it believes in conserving the great constructive achievements of the past. And it will be reactionary if that means reacting against ignorant and reckless efforts to destroy precisely what is most precious in our great economic, political and cultural heritage in the name of alleged "progress."

The number of "concrete" words is zero: the paragraph says just as much or as little as the phrase *passive exercise* in that reducing ad. There *is* a difference, though: the reducing-ad people offered a fuller explanation by telephone, but the editors of *The Freeman* did not.

So don't waste your time and energy on bundles of high-level abstractions. Even more important: don't brood over them. Those big words have a terrible attraction to most of us. We are apt to stare at them and get entangled in such questions as "What is the meaning of life?," "What is truth?" or "Does the universe have a purpose?"

One of the many books on thinking was written by Mr. Henry Hazlitt, the economist and former editorial writer for the *New York Times*. Mr. Hazlitt devotes a whole long chapter to questions about high-level abstractions. With great emphasis, he tells his reader that of all questions, these are the *most useful* to ask. Among his examples are "Is society for the benefit of the individual or is the individual for the benefit of society?", "Is utility a good moral guide?", "What knowledge is of most worth?" and that old standby, "What is truth?"

In another book on thinking you'll find exactly the opposite point of view. It is *The Logic of Modern Physics* by Professor Percy W. Bridgman, Nobel prize winner in physics. Professor Bridgman minces no words. He considers all questions of this sort as examples of sheer verbalism and says they are the *most useless*. In his book, he called them "meaningless questions"; later on, he thought of an even more contemptuous word and called them "footless questions."

As you'll expect by now, I am on the side of Bridgman in this matter. Those big questions are more than useless, they are actually harmful. There is no satisfactory answer to any of them, and we're apt to ask them again and again, with an ever-deepening sense of frustration and failure.

Next time you find yourself wrestling with such a question, stop and translate it into a low-level, concrete question to which you can find an answer. Instead of "What is the meaning of life?" ask yourself "What did I do today, and for what purpose?" Instead of "What knowledge is of most worth?" ask "What did I learn last year and how did I apply it?"

And when it comes to the question "What is truth?", remember that our civilization has developed an elaborate procedure to establish the truth about things and events, namely, a court trial. Yet, no witness has ever been asked to answer the question "What is truth?" More likely, he is asked: "Now tell us exactly what you did between 3:30 and 4:30 on the afternoon of August 4, 1947."

CHAPTER 8

The Rise and Fall of Formal Logic

I appeal to common observation, which has always found these artificial methods of reasoning more adapted to catch and entangle the mind, than to instruct and inform the understanding.
—John Locke, *An Essay Concerning Human Understanding*

Over two thousand years ago, in 366 B.C., the eighteen-year-old son of a prominent Greek physician arrived in Athens and became a student at Plato's Academy. His name was Aristotle. Being exceptionally brilliant, he soon turned from a student into a teacher and eventually stayed at the Academy for twenty years, until Plato died.

Aristotle discovered that philosophy was taught at the Academy in a rather curious way. Instead of lectures, teachers and students played a then fashionable intellectual parlor game—the "yes-or-no" game. The rules of the yes-or-no game were simple: There were two players, one who asked questions and another who answered either yes or no. At the start of the game, the players picked a debating problem—a general question that could be answered by yes or no. One took the yes side, the other the no side. Then the questioner tried to force his opponent into switching sides. He asked a series of questions the opponent had to answer by yes or no. If all the yeses and noes added up to the admission "You are right on the main question," the questioner had won; if he couldn't wrest this admission from his opponent, he had lost.

Plato's *Dialogues* contain innumerable play-by-play descriptions of the yes-and-no game. Take just one example, the Dialogue *Meno*. Socrates and Meno debate the question "Can virtue be taught?" Socrates, the questioner, says yes, Meno says no. The successive moves in the match take up many pages; let's just take a quick look at one game:

> *Socrates:* Does not everyone see that knowledge alone is taught?
> *Meno:* I agree.
> *Socrates:* Then if virtue is knowledge, virtue will be taught?
> *Meno:* Certainly.
> *Socrates:* Then . . . if virtue is of such a nature, it will be taught; and if not, not?
> *Meno:* Certainly.
> *Socrates:* And the next question is, whether virtue is knowledge or of another species?
> *Meno:* Yes. . . .

Socrates wins this game after twenty-four moves. Here is the end game:

> *Socrates:* Is it not true that . . . that which profits is wisdom—and virtue, as we said, is profitable?
> *Meno:* Certainly.
> *Socrates:* And thus . . . virtue . . . is wisdom?
> *Meno:* . . . Very true.
> *Socrates:* But if this is true, then the good are not by nature good?
> *Meno:* I think not.
> *Socrates:* But if the good are not by nature good, are they made good by instruction?
> *Meno* (conceding he has lost): There is no other alternative, Socrates. On the supposition that virtue is knowledge, there can be no doubt that virtue is taught.

By the time Aristotle arrived on the scene, the yes-or-no game was almost a hundred years old. All sorts of variations and tricks had been invented; hardly anybody played it any more in the pure classical style of Socrates. In the Dialogue *Euthydemus*, Plato gives an example of what happened to the once noble game. A rhetoric teacher, Dionysodorus, plays it with a young man, Ctesippus.

> *Dionysodorus:* If you will answer my questions . . . You say you have a dog?
> *Ctesippus:* Yes . . .
> *Dionysodorus:* And he has puppies?
> *Ctesippus:* Yes . . .
> *Dionysodorus:* And the dog is the father of them?
> *Ctesippus:* Yes . . .
> *Dionysodorus:* And his is not yours?
> *Ctesippus:* To be sure he is.

Dionysodorus: Then he is a father, and his is yours; ergo, he is your father, and the puppies are your brothers. . . . Let me ask you one little question more: You beat this dog?

Ctesippus: Indeed I do . . .

Dionysodorus: Then you beat your father.

Aristotle, the new young teacher, was appalled by this situation. He wondered what could be done about it. Then he realized that in all those years nobody had ever bothered to write down the rules of the game. Maybe that was it; maybe the original beautiful game could be restored if someone formulated the rules for playing it properly. Aristotle seized his opportunity and composed the first book of rules for the game. Later he wrote several more. Together, they formed a complete manual of elementary and advanced yes-or-no playing.

And that, in a nutshell, is the story of the origin of formal logic.

I know that this sounds unbelievable. It's downright shocking to think that formal logic, "the science of thinking," started out as a set of rules for what amounts to an intellectual parlor game. But there isn't the slightest doubt about it: all scholars agree that that's the historical truth. Almost sixty years ago, Professor William Minto, in his textbook on logic, put the matter this way:

> Aristotle's *Logic* in its primary aim was as practical as a treatise on navigation or *Cavendish on Whist.* The latter is the more exact of the two comparisons. It was in effect in its various parts a series of handbooks for a temporarily fashionable intellectual game, a peculiar mode of disputation or dialectic, the game of Question and Answer, the game so fully illustrated in the *Dialogues* of Plato, the game identified with the name of Socrates. [Today, of course, we have to read *Culbertson on Bridge* instead of *Cavendish on Whist.*]

If you want a more recent statement on the matter, you'll find it in great detail in Ernst Kapp's *Greek Foundations of Traditional Logic,* published in 1942.

Mind you, I am not saying that formal logic is necessarily trivial just because it was originally derived from a game. Games are often excellent starting points for the analysis of complex problems. Pascal created the theory of probability in 1654, trying to answer some questions put to him by a gambler, the Chevalier de Méré. And a few years ago, von Neumann and Morgenstern developed a brand-new economic theory by analyzing the behavior around a poker table. So the parlor-game history of formal logic in itself is no argument against it.

But there are other arguments against it, and they are pretty serious.

For one thing, there's the awkward fact that the yes-or-no game went out of fashion some two thousand years ago. Maybe formal logic would be still practical as training for the mind if people played yes-or-no as much as they play canasta or bridge. But they don't; and it's hard to teach the rules of a game to those who aren't interested in playing it. It's like trying to get a baseball fan interested in cricket.

What's more, the rules are quite confusing if you don't know the nature of the game. Take the centerpiece of the whole system, Aristotle's famous categorical syllogism. The standard example in all textbooks is this:

> All men are mortal.
> Socrates is a man.
> Therefore Socrates is mortal.

Now this is clear enough if you know the game. Then it means: "If you want to force your opponent to concede a proposition like 'Socrates is mortal,' ask him first 'Are all men mortal?' and then 'Is Socrates a man?' After answering yes to both questions, he'll have to say yes to the third one too."

But if you don't know the game, the syllogism is apt to mean something entirely different to you. If you don't know that it is a *technique of driving someone else to a foregone conclusion*, you'll naturally assume that it is a way of arriving at a conclusion by yourself. You'll look at the syllogism as a model for solitary thinking. You'll believe that you *ought* to think like this: "Is Socrates mortal? Well, now, let me see. Let's take it for granted that all men are mortal. And, of course, Socrates is a man . . . Why, that proves it, doesn't it? Socrates is mortal."

The result can be quite disastrous. Take, for instance, the best popular book on formal logic, *How to Think Straight* by Robert H. Thouless. At the end of the book, Mr. Thouless gives the reader a number of reasoning tests. His instructions are: "Read the argument and consider whether it is a sound or unsound argument. . . . An argument is sound if the conclusion follows necessarily from the statements that have gone before it." Here are three of his tests:

All poisonous things are bitter. Arsenic is not bitter. Therefore, arsenic is not poisonous.

Every woman is a potential mother, and no one possessing this sacred potentiality is capable of committing crimes of the worst kind. It follows from this that none of the worst criminals are women.

All true Americans have a marked sense of humor. This sense of humor is noticeably lacking in all Communists. So no true American can be a Communist.

In the key to the tests, Mr. Thouless quite properly marks all these arguments as sound—according to the rules of formal logic. And so they are: if a yes-or-no player has said yes to the first two statements, he has to admit the third.

But it would be a great mistake to accept these arguments as models of sound thinking. A sound thinker, upon hearing or reading that "all poisonous things are bitter," would say "Now *wait* a minute" and stop right there. He would do the same thing with each of the other unwarranted assumptions. If he didn't, and meekly accepted them "for the sake of the argument," he would be an utterly correct yes-or-no player, but a pretty poor thinker.

So formal logic detached from the yes-or-no game is useless and even dangerous. It's an unnatural way of thinking, a contrived technique of going from unwarranted assumptions to foregone conclusions.

All this isn't new. It has been said hundreds of times for hundreds of years. In 1690, John Locke wrote:

He that will look into many parts of Asia and America, will find men reason there perhaps as acutely as himself, who yet never heard of a syllogism, nor can reduce any one argument to those forms: and I believe scarce anyone makes syllogisms in reasoning within himself. God has not been so sparing to men to make them barely two-legged creatures, and left it to Aristotle to make them rational. . . . Syllogism comes after knowledge, and then a man has little or no need of it.

And Francis Bacon wrote:

The present system of logic rather assists in confirming and rendering inveterate the errors found on vulgar notions than in searching after truth, and is therefore more hurtful than useful.

Among modern psychologists I quote Max Wertheimer who has found formal logic "barren, boring, empty, unproductive." Or George Humphrey, who tried to collect specimens of syllogistic thinking in real life. All he came up with was a single nasty answer given by a garage mechanic to a customer's question: "How does my starter work?" The mechanic answered with a perfect syllogism: "Your car is a '42 Plymouth. All '42 Plymouths have manually-operated starters. Yours is manually operated." That statement obviously was not made in the spirit of Socrates.

All of which, I hope, shows why this book does *not* include the basic rules of formal logic. I know, of course, that formal logic is taught at every university in the land, and that it is dealt with in almost every book on thinking. But I honestly believe that you're better off without it. Most psychologists today would say the same.

However, let's not leave the subject yet. The history of the two-thousand-year reign of formal logic has a fascinating epilogue—the development of *symbolic* logic.

This brings us to George Boole, an Englishman who lived about a hundred years ago. Boole had the bright idea that the Aristotelian system was nothing but a sort of mathematics of thinking; what it needed was some simple formulas, so that one could work with *a, b* and *c* instead of shuffling and reshuffling those stale old examples of all men being mortal and Socrates being a man. Whereupon Boole translated the complicated system of formal logic into streamlined Boolean algebra.

Boolean algebra took a long while to take hold, but it finally did, in a way that would have surprised George Boole if he had lived to see it. On the basis of his work, a tremendous system of mathematical or symbolic logic was gradually built up, climaxing in the monumental *Principia Mathematica* by Russell and Whitehead, published in 1910. By then, Aristotle's original system was already dwarfed by all the rest of the new science of symbolic logic. By 1937, when Professor Susanne K. Langer published her *Introduction to Symbolic Logic*, Aristotle had to be content with a little spot in the appendix. "Thousands of men, through thousands of years, have had millions of headaches over Aristotle's system of logic," Professor Langer writes, explaining that with symbolic logic it can be reduced to three sets of equations. And after three more lines with the three sets of equations there follows the calm announcement: "For a true Aristotelian this exhausts the abstract system of logic."

I am not going to confuse you here with the three sets of equations and their strange symbolism, but I *will* try to show you the first set in familiar mathematical form. Let's say that *a* stands for *Socrates, b* for *man,* and *c* for *mortal.* Then we have:

$$b \times (-c) = 0$$
$$a \times (-b) = 0$$
$$\overline{}$$
$$a \times (-c) = 0$$

Which means:

> Men not mortal equal zero (i.e. there *are* none)
> Socrates not a man equals zero (i.e. he *is* one)
> Socrates not mortal equals zero (i.e. he must be mortal)

In other words:

> All men are mortal
> Socrates is a man
> Socrates is mortal

I hope this will give you a general idea of how symbolic logic works. There's nothing mysterious about it; in fact, Boolean algebra is much simpler than ordinary high school algebra. The kids would love it if they could take it instead.

Now the question arises: What is symbolic logic good for? If formal logic were practical for everyday thinking, then naturally symbolic logic would be a handy thing to do the job more effectively. But you have seen that formal logic won't do you much good with ordinary problems; and the same, I'm afraid, is true of symbolic logic.

However, not all of life's problems are ordinary, and symbolic logic has its uses. It has been shown, for instance, that it is practical when you have to solve the following problem in an examination:

Certain data obtained from a study of a group of 1000 employees in a cotton mill as to their race, sex, and marital state were unofficially reported as follows: 525 colored lives; 312 male lives; 470 married lives; 42 colored males; 147 married colored; 86 married males; 25 married colored males. Test this classification to determine whether the numbers reported in the various groups are consistent.

Symbolic logic helps to show that these data are inconsistent.

In the last few years, symbolic logic has really come into its own in the operation of electronic computing machines. These robots solve problems only when they are translated into machine language; and a mathematician must know symbolic logic to do the translations properly. Without symbolic logic it would be practically impossible to feed a problem to a machine. And since these mathematical machines have great possibilities, symbolic logic will soon be recognized as a highly important science.

And so we see that formal logic has come full circle: From the rules of an ancient parlor game, it developed into a system that dominated Western thinking for two thousand years—and then wound up as technique for feeding problems into automatic machines.

CHAPTER 9

How Not to Be Bamboozled

I realized that regardless of persons or topics of discussion the same tricks and dodges recurred again and again and could easily be recognized.
—Schopenhauer, *On Logic and Dialectic*

Way, way back in Cohen and Nagel's four-hundred-page textbook on logic, you'll find five measly pages on logical fallacies. If you are like most people, this will surprise you: logic, to you, is primarily a technique for spotting fallacies. But that's not the way logicians look at it. To them, logic is syllogisms, immediate inference, and a dozen other things; the detection of fallacies is a vulgar preoccupation of laymen—the kind of people who are interested in grocery bills rather than fine points of economic theory.

However, logicians weren't always so squeamish about the popular aspects of their science. Aristotle didn't hesitate to put convenient tags on recurrent fallacies (after all, he wrote a practical debate-game handbook); and his ancient and medieval followers added to the list. There is a stately air of pillars and togas about these Latin phrases:

> *argumentum ad hominem*
> *argumentum ad populum*
> *argumentum ad misericordiam*
> *argumentum ad baculum*
> *argumentum ad crumenam*
> *argumentum ad verecundiam*
> *argumentum ad ignorantiam*
> *argumentum ad captandum vulgus*

But of course the measured Latin organ tones are misleading. This is a list of cheap tricks. The *argumentum ad hominem* is an appeal to personal prejudice; *ad populum* means an appeal to mass emotions, *ad misericordiam* means the exploitation of pity, *ad baculum* is the appeal to brute force ("to the club"), *ad crumenam* the appeal to money ("to the purse"), *ad verecundiam* the playing up of prestige, *ad ignorantiam* the stress upon ignorance, and *ad captandum vulgus* a catch-all term for any dishonest argument "to catch the crowd."

The logicians traditionally use examples from debating. Today it is more instructive to use examples from advertising. Let's imagine an advertising campaign for "Durtee Soap," and examples for each of the Latin tags will suggest themselves. An *argumentum ad hominem* might be: "Look at yourself in the mirror; only Durtee Soap will get you real clean." *Ad populum:* "The easiest way to be loved by everybody is to use Durtee Soap." *Ad misericordiam:* "Don't make your children unhappy by not washing their ears with Durtee Soap." *Ad baculum:* "Durtee Soap is being advertised every hour on the hour on all major networks." *Ad crumenam:* "Durtee Soap costs 2 per cent less and is 50 per cent more floatable than any other soap." *Ad verecundiam:* "All five Rockefeller boys were brought up exclusively on Durtee Soap." *Ad ignorantiam:* "Only Durtee Soap contains the miracle ingredient Lodahocum. If you've never heard of Lodahocum, you ought to be ashamed of yourself." *Ad captandum vulgus:* "Durtee Soap is the favorite of everybody from coast to coast."

Naturally I tried to make my examples funny. But the sober truth is that they are essentially no different from all the advertising we see around us every day.

However, the eight Latin phrases that I gave you aren't all the logical fallacies there are—not by a long shot. There are lots more listed in the logic books, many of them with such forbidding names as *undistributed middle, ignoratio elenchi,* or *a dicto simpliciter ad dictum secundum quid.* Schopenhauer wrote that he collected about forty of these debating stratagems in order to write a book about them, but got so disgusted with all those underhanded devices that he gave up the project. In our own time, Professor Robert H. Thouless performed the same kind of job in the book *How to Think Straight,* which I mentioned before. His list contains thirty-four "dishonest tricks."

All these catalogues and classifications are fascinating and full of entertainment of a mild, intellectual sort. But they are not practical for everyday purposes. Nobody can live in today's world of propaganda

and advertising and carefully label everything he hears or sees in
thirty-four different ways. What you need to defend yourself is fewer
labels rather than more.

A few years ago, the Institute for Propaganda Analysis tried to do
something about that and came up with a list of seven propaganda
devices. Here they are:

1. Name calling
2. Glittering generality
3. Transfer
4. Testimonial
5. Plain folks
6. Card stacking
7. Band wagon

You can easily see that these are the old Latin tags in modern dress.
"Name calling" is the *argumentum ad hominem*, "glittering generality,"
"transfer" and "testimonial" are all subcategories of *ad verecundiam*,
"plain folks" and "band wagon" are both *ad populum*. "Card stacking"
isn't really a fallacy at all, but simply a way of lying.

I know from my own experience that even these seven phrases are
hard to remember. (Besides, they don't cover everything.) So let's see
whether we can whittle down the list some more.

To do that, let's go back to the textbooks and see whether the fallacies fall into any large, easily remembered groups. They do: All texts
agree that there are formal, verbal and material fallacies.

Formal fallacies we can dispose of very quickly. They have to do
with the correct application of the syllogism technique—in other words,
with violations of the rules for the yes-or-no game. Since that game
isn't played any longer by the advertisers, propagandists and other mass
producers of fallacies, we'll just skip those.

Verbal fallacies have to do with the tricky use of words. To defend
ourselves against those, we have to remember what we know about
language and words—particularly the difference between abstract words
and concrete words, such as names, numbers and dates.

This leaves us with the material fallacies, of which there are two
kinds: you either bring up a point that is irrelevant or leave out a
point that is relevant. Usually they differ in their language level: irrelevant points are apt to be in concrete terms, aiming at personal interests,
emotions and prejudices; and omissions of relevant points are usually
disguised by high, wide and unspecific language. In other words, the

advertiser or propagandist is apt to use general terms when he should be specific, and specific terms when he is trying to distract your attention.

The most practical defense against fallacies is therefore to use two labels, one for irrelevant points that should be dismissed and one for relevant points that are missing. Let's keep these labels simple. Let's call one of them "So what?" and the other "Specify."

Is this an oversimplification? You may call it that; but the point is that it works. Armed with "So what?" and "Specify," you can catch practically all fallacious advertising and propaganda.

"So what?" ads are perhaps more common than "Specify" ads. Advertisers love the *argumentum ad verecundiam* (prestige) and we are told day in day out who uses what. Rita Hayworth uses Pan-Stik (So what?), Ava Gardner uses Lux (So what?), the Countess of Carnarvon uses Angel Face Make-Up (So what?), and Mrs. John A. Roosevelt, Mrs. George Jay Gould, Jr., Lady Bridgett Poulett, the Duchess de Richelieu, Miss Nancy du Pont, and Mrs. Francis Grover Cleveland all use Pond's (So what?); Grantland Rice drinks Rheingold (So what?), Pat O'Brien drinks Schaefer's (So what?), Gary Cooper drinks Pabst (So what?), Victor McLaglen drinks Blatz (So what?), and Louis Bromfield, Adolphe Menjou, Jesse Lasky, Danton Walker and Fulton Lewis, Jr. are all men of distinction and you know what *they* drink (So what?). And then, of course, there are the well-known preferences of Miss Rheingold, Betty Crocker, Li'l Abner and Elsie the Cow.

"Specify" ads are all those that refer in general terms to the qualities or indirect effects of a product. Advertisers, for example, never specify why you should drink one whisky rather than another. One is "America's mildest," another is "gentle in taste," a third has "good taste through the years," a fourth is "of the very finest flavor and quality," a fifth is "perfection in every glass," a sixth "has no substitute," a seventh is "your key to hospitality," an eighth is the "center of attraction," a ninth is labeled "quality tells," and a tenth is good because "there is nothing better in the market."

"Specify how" is also the answer to all those ads that promise a tremendous return in erotic pleasures for a small investment. Here is one:

> If people shy away from you
> Because bad breath's your Waterloo
> Just chew B-Wise, and you will be
> The man of pop-u-lar-i-ty!
> For kissable breath . . . B-Wise Gum 5¢

Here is another:

A moment bright with rapture. Winged ecstasy set to shimmering music. You're whirling through space, *lost . . .* yet you've just found yourself for the first time! This is love, love, love. . . . It's so easy with Woodbury Facial Soap.

The perfume ads, of course, have become a standard gag. One perfume "makes you want to fall in love," another is "drumming in his heart . . . burning in his soul," a third is the "potent essence of desire to touch." A fourth, Black Panther, is described this way:

The slumbering fire of Black Panther attacks a man's heart—attacks a woman's—until the two hearts merge in a flame of ecstasy. Wear this new perfume for an unforgettable evening . . . but only if you dare risk the danger and dark delight of stirring primitive emotions. At all ten-cent stores.

But all these ads, you'll say, hardly make an argument worth thinking about. The fact is, few ads do. Only once in a while an ad appears that really deserves logical analysis. One of those is a television dealers' ad that appeared in November, 1950, newspapers and made quite a stir. All over the country letters to the editor and editorials said it was "offensive," "blackmail," "cruel pressure," "in bad taste," and "unmitigated nonsense." Why did people care? What got them so excited? What made the ad so powerfully effective? Let's see:

THERE ARE SOME THINGS A SON OR DAUGHTER WON'T TELL YOU!

"Aw gee, pop, why can't we get a television set?" You've heard that. But there's more you won't hear. *Do you expect a seven-year-old to find words for the deep loneliness he's feeling?*

He may complain—"The kids were mean and wouldn't play with me!" Do you expect him to blurt out the truth—*that he's really ashamed to be with the gang—that he feels left out because he doesn't see the television shows they see, know the things they know?*

You can tell someone about a bruised finger. How can a little girl describe a bruise deep inside? *No, your daughter won't ever tell you the humiliation she's felt in begging those precious hours of television from a neighbor.*

You give your child's *body* all the sunshine and fresh air and vitamins you can. *How about sunshine for his morale? How about vitamins for his mind?* Educators agree—television is all that and more for a growing child.

When television means so much more to a child than entertainment alone, can you deny it to your family any longer?

Is this a persuasive argument? You bet it is. When I read it, I had three small children in the house and no television set. The ad was aimed straight at me and I could feel its hot breath in full force.

But if you are armed with the weapons of "So what?" and "Specify," even a powerful ad like this won't hurt you. First you take the main appeal—the children's complaints—and classify that. It's a pure *argumentum ad misericordiam* (arousal of pity): with the ad went a picture of a sad boy and a girl in tears. The answer is: So what? So what if your small children pester you to buy a television set? Do they know anything about what is involved? Do they have the judgment to assess the quality of television programs? Do they have the experience to compare them with other forms of entertainment? Do they know anything about the cost of a television set? Do they know what it would do to the family budget? The answer to all these questions is clearly no. Of course they are after you to buy a set, just as they want a lot of other expensive things that happen to catch their fancy. But so what?

And now let's ask the advertisers to specify their statements. Specify the percentage of children who feel humiliated because they see television at the neighbors'. Specify what research produced those data. Specify just how important all this is for the child's morale. Specify what you mean by "vitamins for the child's mind." Specify those television programs that fit this classification. Specify the ratio of those programs to all others. Specify the programs that are *not* vitamins for the minds of children. Specify how many of those other programs children are apt to look at. Finally, specify what you mean by "educators agree." All of them? If not all, how many? Who are they? Where do they teach? On what basis have they arrived at their opinions? Exactly what do they recommend? Specify.

By the time you have raised all these questions, the ad has crumbled into nothing. Of course, you may still decide to buy a television set, but it makes all the difference whether you arrive at your decision by exercising your own mind or by falling for someone else's specious reasoning.

Can other forms of persuasion be tackled in the same way? They certainly can, and it's a far more important job than self-protection against advertising. After all, advertising is *labeled* advertising; you're somewhat protected because you know someone is trying to sell you something. Other things are more dangerous: they come as information or entertainment and it's up to you to recognize them for what they are.

Examples aren't hard to find; but when a national magazine carries an attack against a twelve-year-old federal law, that's unusual. The following excerpt is from an article challenging certain applications of the Fair Labor Standards Act (which forbids the employment of children under sixteen, especially near heavy machinery). The author is a small-town printer and publisher who was caught violating the law. He complains that he has been forced to replace children with an expensive machine. (To make it easy for you, I put "So what's" and "Specify's" in their proper places.)

Recently . . . a man with a face like a beaked eagle [So what?] and with a bulging brief case [So what?] edged in [So what?] . . . He was from the Department of Labor to make a check . . .
. . . The office door crashed open, and in roared twenty-six kids ranging from nineteen years down to seven . . . He asked: "What are these?"
I started to tell him . . . A gang from the high school always dropped in after school, and we usually let five or six [Specify exact number, ages, and frequency of employment] join the folding party [Specify at what wages] and gave them cider, cookies, radio programs and lots of chatter [So what?] for two or three hours, two days a week [Specify exact periods].
"It's sort of a private youth movement," my wife explained. [Specify what it consists of.] "When they're not in here, many of them are running loose in the streets, getting into all kinds of trouble [So what?]. Here they earn some money and . . . have a good time [So what?]."

It isn't always possible to go beyond "So what?" and "Specify" and supply the facts missing in the argument. In this case, however, the data were available and so I could rewrite the excerpt for you, leaving out all the irrelevant stuff and specifying what wasn't specified. Now it reads like this:

Recently a man from the Department of Labor came to make a check.
. . . The office door crashed open, and in roared twenty-six kids ranging from nineteen years down to seven. He asked: "What are these?"
I started to tell him: A gang from the high school always dropped in after school, and we regularly employed ten boys under sixteen to fold papers. One of them was eleven, two were twelve, three were thirteen, and four were fourteen. Their wages ranged from 16¢ to 35¢ an hour. One fourteen-year-old worked evenings until 11:30, another thirteen-year-old until 11:00.
"It's sort of a private youth movement," my wife explained, "consisting of work for children under sixteen."

This is a rather simple example of how to tackle a challenging piece of writing.

The battle against propaganda is a more serious business. Fortunately you live in a country where propaganda comes from all sides, so that to some extent it cancels each other out. If you lived in a totalitarian country, you would know how hard it is to keep up the daily fight against one-sided propaganda, trying desperately to keep your head above the sea of fallacious arguments.

What makes the struggle so hard is the fact that the totalitarians' strongest weapon is not logical, but psychological: the tremendous power of repetition. After the steady hammering of their propaganda machine, millions of Germans were sincerely surprised when they learned after the last war that New York had *not* been bombed to ruins and that Roosevelt's real name was *not* Rosenfeld. (If you doubt the power of sheer repetition, try to consider rationally the questions whether Chesterfields are strong or whether Lucky Strike means medium tobacco.)

The totalitarians soon discovered that repetition is effective, regardless of whether you use it with fallacies or just plain lies. In fact, they found that the bigger the lies, the more powerful the effect—they invented the technique of the Big Lie.

I can't offer you any protection against lies, because there is none. If my publishers told you that 4,562 junior executives were made vice-presidents immediately after reading this book, you might believe the statement or not; but you'd have no way of telling offhand whether it was a lie or whether there was anything to it.

One thing you *can* do, though: you can consider the source of any statement that is used as part of an argument. If it comes from an interested source, then you have a right to suspect it; in fact, you'd better make it your business to suspect it.

In particular, make it your business to suspect what a member of a group tells you about the wishes and attitudes of another: *Beware of the wrong spokesman*. Don't believe grownups who tell you that children love spinach, wives who insist that husbands like pastels and chintz, Democrats who are sure Republicans despise their own candidates, whites who explain that Negroes prefer segregation, businessmen who announce that labor wants to get rid of unions, employers who tell you that small boys love to work.

George Orwell, the late author of *1984*, wrote in an essay about Edward Lear's poems:

> While the Pobble was in the water some unidentified creatures come and ate his toes off, and when he got home his aunt remarked:
> >It's a fact the whole world knows,
> >That Pobbles are happier without their toes,

which is funny because it has a meaning, and one might even say a political significance. For the whole theory of authoritarian government is summed up in the statement that Pobbles are happier without their toes.

CHAPTER 10

Why Argue?

It is always better to say right out what you think without trying to prove anything much: for all our proofs are only variations of our opinions, and the contrary-minded listen neither to one nor the other.

—Goethe

Logic is the science of argument.

This was true in the fourth century B.C., when Aristotle started it all; it is still true today, when the teaching of logic is being justified by the fact that it helps students win an argument.

But what does it mean—"win an argument"? Let's return from our side-trip into logic, advertising and propaganda, and remember the basic facts about thinking.

Thinking is the manipulation of memory traces in your brain. Your thinking is the fruit of your life experience; the patterns in your brain are your own and nobody else's.

When you argue with someone, you pit your organization of nerve patterns against his. Your opinion is the result of past experience; so is his. If you win the argument, it means that your opponent has to realign his nerve patterns so that they parallel yours.

This is unpleasant for him. Everybody's established opinions are as comfortable as an old shoe; they have acquired exactly the right shape and form through continued use in all sorts of conditions. If you are forced to accept a different opinion, it's like getting used to a new pair of shoes: the change may be for the better, but it's always a somewhat uncomfortable experience.

Winning an argument is therefore, to begin with, doing something unpleasant to someone else.

But does that matter, you say, if you are right and the other fellow is wrong? Well, does it? Let's take a simple example. Someone has used the quotation from *The Ancient Mariner,* "Water, water everywhere, and not a drop to drink." Knowing better, you speak up and say that it is ". . . nor any drop to drink." An argument follows and, with the aid of Bartlett's *Familiar Quotations,* you win. Your opponent is embarrassed. Was it worth doing that to him? Is the truth so important?

Oh well, you say, that's a trivial example—an argument turning on a simple question of fact. What about really significant arguments about deep-going differences of opinion? Aren't such arguments worth winning?

All right, let's take another example from literature—a famous controversy this time. Not long ago, I was reading the letters of Maxwell Perkins, the late, great editor of Thomas Wolfe, Ernest Hemingway, and F. Scott Fitzgerald. I came upon the sentence: "It is certain, to my mind, that the man Shakespeare was not the author of what we consider Shakespeare's works." Suppose you belong to the minority Perkins belonged to, and find yourself in an argument with an orthodox Shakespearean. What would happen if you won that argument?

Naturally, your opponent would resent it terrifically. You'd have upset many of his most cherished beliefs, you'd have made his mind acutely uncomfortable, you'd have filled his brain with sore spots.

And after some time, it would turn out that you haven't won the argument after all. Your opponent's old, strongly held ideas would gradually overcome all your arguments, by and by the balance would be restored, and his mind would settle back in the old grooves. If you won the argument because of your logically trained, superior debater's technique, this would happen even sooner. "Why," your opponent would say to himself, "that fellow put something over on me. Everybody knows that all this business about Shakespeare not being the author of Shakespeare's plays is nonsense. Can't understand what came over me when I agreed with all that stuff."

The trouble is, you see, that big questions cannot be settled by looking up the facts; you may be able to win an *argument* about a big question, but you'll hardly ever win a *person* over to your side. (Even facts won't always do the trick: plenty of people would still believe in Shakespeare's genius if it were proved that he never wrote a line.)

Of course, I'm not talking here about arguments you are trying to win for a purpose: if you are out to make a sale, that's a different matter. Or if you are out for votes. Or if you want to win a law suit (I'll go into that in the next chapter). In all those cases it will obviously profit you to win your argument and hold on to your point of view regardless. Probably, in one way or another, you'll use those ancient tricks for fitting *your* brain patterns into established patterns in your opponent's mind ("You believe in vitamins for your child's body—how about vitamins for his mind?" . . . "It's sort of a private youth movement . . ."). And your opponent, if he is smart, will try to fend you off.

But when it comes to purposeless argument, argument for argument's sake, that's something else again. There's no profit at all in hanging on to your point of view for dear life, just because it's yours. It's not as precious as all that.

Most dinner-table or living-room arguments are hardly arguments at all. You stick to one opinion because it's been part of your mental furniture for years, and the other fellow sticks to another for the same reason.

Conversations of this sort aren't taken down in shorthand, which makes it hard to give examples. But "sidewalk interviews" by newspaper photographers are a reasonable substitute. Here is one from the New York *Post*:*

Question: Who are the biggest gossips—men or women?

Miss Florence C. (bookkeeper): The men are the biggest gossips. They can't keep anything under their hats. They are always telling their friends the things that they should keep to themselves. And women are the main topic they gossip about.

Dr. Max O. (dentist): The men have the women beat by far. They are always talking about the other fellow's business life. And many times by their tales they put a man in an awkward situation.

Miss Jean P. (division manager): Both of them are just as petty and gossipy. I wait on them all day long and I know. There is no difference in either sex. Both men and women gossip to me about things I never should be told or even know about.

Mr. Pasquale T. (barber): The feminine sex takes the prize on that subject. They are always chattering. They don't need a hint of anything, just let them surmise something and they are capable of building it into nice juicy gossip.

Mrs. Maureen M. (housewife): Women definitely. They have a tendency to be very jealous and will gossip about other women whether it is necessary or not. Just give them the opportunity and they'll never miss it.

* Reproduced from the New York *Post* of September 18, 1950. Copyright 1950 New York *Post* Corp.

Imagine these people sitting in a living room and you have the perfect pattern of an ordinary conversational argument. A general question is raised and five people give five different answers—each according to his or her experience or general pattern of living. The girl who works in an office remembers all the men she has heard gossiping about women, the girl who waits on customers meets men and women gossips all day long, the housewife recalls the chatter at canasta games, the barber has listened to women under the dryer, and the dentist sums up *his* experience with anguished, open-mouthed businessmen. If these people started to argue among themselves, they would each repeat and elaborate what they have said. After a while, the argument might get heated—Mrs. M. insisting that only a married woman really knows anything about gossip, Dr. O. announcing that only a dentist can arrive at a detached, objective point of view on the subject, and so on. Is it possible for anyone to win the argument? Hardly. The question could only be settled by a complete statistical survey—and even then you'd have trouble defining a gossip and agreeing on what makes one gossip bigger than another. For all practical purposes, the question is unanswerable and to argue about it is rather silly.

Now you are protesting against my choice of an example. Of course, you say, these are idle, aimless arguments. But there are topics worth talking about, and people who are intelligent and well-informed. Should *all* arguments be dismissed as useless?

Before I answer that question, let me give you a few more examples— serious arguments this time, debates between experts. The first deals with the newspaper I have just been quoting, the New York *Post*. In 1949 that paper was taken over by a new young editor, Mr. James A. Wechsler, who successfully built up circulation by a heavy dose of crime and sex. Many old readers of the *Post* were disgusted by the sudden switch. In June, 1950, the *Saturday Review of Literature* ran a lengthy debate between Mr. Wechsler and Mr. August Heckscher, editorial writer on the New York *Herald Tribune*. Mr. Wechsler said that you can't get an audience without using showmanship; Mr. Heckscher said that was "a false formula."

Nobody reading that debate could possibly say that either of the two men won the argument; each stated his point of view, presented excellent reasons in support of it, and proved that he knew what he was talking about. But in the end it was clear that the basic patterns of experience of the two debaters simply couldn't be reconciled.

Mr. Wechsler faced the job of selling a New Dealish paper to millions of potential readers who strangely preferred papers with whose political views they disagreed. He looked at the circulation figures of New York City papers and found the answer to his problem: "The meaning of these numbers is not mysterious. They prove beyond dispute that newspapers which displayed the deepest interest in crimes of passion and passionate crimes have remained far out in front in New York. . . ." His business was to sell a liberal newspaper to liberal readers in Manhattan, Brooklyn and the Bronx. To do that, he had to put sex on page one.

Mr. Heckscher felt that emphasis on sex degraded a paper, regardless of what it printed on the editorial page. He made an excellent case for his point of view. But the telling sentence that gave flavor to his whole argument was one that was obviously based on direct experience:

If friends of the *Post* object to the emphasis of sex, it is on the practical grounds that they do not like being compelled to leave their favorite evening newspaper on the train, or otherwise dispose of it, before entering homes where growing children are entitled to be protected against at least the most brutal and the most sordid facts of life.

Let's turn to another debate which appeared in *The New Yorker*. On one side we have Mr. Lewis Mumford, well-known authority on city planning, contending that the new housing developments in New York City are bad because they add to congestion. Over on the other side is Mr. Herman T. Stichman, New York State Commissioner of Housing, defending the projects because they are what people want. Again, the argument can be reduced to two irreconcilable pictures in the minds of the debaters.

Writes Mr. Stichman:

By and large, Americans appear to aspire to high buildings as the Swiss do to mountains, and to love to congregate in groups . . . If all our tall business and residential structures were to be replaced by buildings of two and three stories, New York City would stretch from here to Hartford. . . . Actually people are commuting almost that far today in their eagerness to enjoy the view from an office on the fortieth floor in Manhattan when they might just as well be doing business on the ground floor of a building on Main Street in their home towns. What we need is not better planners but better psychologists to help us understand why people are so gregarious and why they seek the heights.

Answers Mr. Mumford:

Mr. Stichman says that the people of New York have a passionate desire for high buildings. That singular passion exists only in the minds of the authorities. . . . Every honest poll of housing preferences shows that the popular ideal for people with families is single-family houses with a patch of garden around them, an ideal for the sake of which people who can afford it put up with the all but intolerable handicaps of commuting.

I think that Mr. Mumford has a slight edge in this argument, just as I think that Mr. Heckscher had a slight edge in the other one. After all, neither Mr. Stichman nor Mr. Wechsler were disinterested debaters: one defended his agency, the other his paper. So the pictures in their minds were necessarily biased. But the fact remains that an argument of this sort cannot really be won. A man who sees people attracted by skyscrapers like moths by a flame can't convince another who sees the picture of a little bungalow etched in each heart.

In our next example we can safely say that both sides are completely disinterested. Here are two academicians debating a question in *Science* magazine. One is Dr. Bernhard J. Stern, a Columbia University sociologist, the other is Dr. Curt Stern, a University of California biologist. The argument is over the old question of heredity *vs.* environment— more specifically, over the low birth rate among higher-income people and whether it means that our nation is in danger of getting more stupid. Dr. Curt Stern of California thinks there may be something to this, Dr. Bernhard J. Stern of Columbia thinks not. The remarkable thing is that both base their conclusions on exactly the same data: the results of intelligence tests.

Stern of Columbia is not impressed at all by differentials in intelligence tests.

The tests, [he says] use chiefly words, situations, pictures, and experiences which are much more familiar to individuals who have grown up in middle and upper socio-economic groups. The conventional tests measure, therefore, not the real intelligence of the child or adult, but the cultural and economic opportunities they have had.

Stern of California thinks otherwise.

Even with these imperfections of the tests in mind, the results strongly suggest hereditary influence. . . . I found it hard to avoid the conclusion that there *are* differences in the genetic endowment of the different socio-economic groups.

And there the argument comes to a standstill. The two Sterns look at the same figures and graphs; one thinks something may have to be done about differences in our birth rate, the other sees the need to provide more educational opportunities for the poor.

Finally, an example I ran into the other day when I bought the latest revision of H. G. Wells' thirty-year-old *Outline of History*. The introduction tells how the original edition was written, how Wells called in four eminent authorities to help him—Sir Ray Lankester, Professor Gilbert Murray, Sir Harry Johnston, and Mr. Ernest Barker—and how they ran into innumerable differences of opinion, which found their way into a mass of footnotes. Mind you, these were not differences as to facts, but *different ways of looking at the same facts*.

Wells, for instance, thought that Napoleon I was of the quality of Mussolini and intellectually inferior to Napoleon III. Mr. Barker disagreed. "Put me down of the opposite opinion," he wrote.

Wells wrote that Athens wasn't a democracy in the modern sense. "The modern idea, that anyone in the state should be a citizen, would have shocked the privileged democrats of Athens profoundly." A footnote adds: "I feel strongly that the text is unjust to Athens. E.B."

Wells tells of the wretched social conditions in Africa in the days of the late Roman Empire. "Manifestly," he writes, "the Vandals came in as a positive relief to such a system." A footnote reads: "E.B. disagrees with this view. He regards it as the pro-Teutonic view of the German historians."

Later in the book, Wells writes about eighteenth-century England. "The poetry, painting, architecture, and imaginative literature of later eighteenth-century England is immeasurably below that of the seventeenth century." There is a footnote signed G.M. (Gilbert Murray): "But Sir Joshua Reynolds, Hogarth, Gray, Gibbon for instance! And the golden age of the great cabinet-makers!" A footnote to the footnote is signed H.G.W.: "Exactly! Culture taking refuge in the portraits, libraries and households of a few rich people. No national culture in the court, nor among the commonalty; a steady decay."

What do all these examples prove? That it's always futile to argue? Not quite. Only that the same facts often create different patterns in different people's brains, and that it's extremely hard to change them—even if you have all the facts at your finger tips and are a whiz in the technique of debating.

Yet I am not going to end this chapter by telling you that you should never argue. Arguing is too much fun for that. Why shouldn't you jump into the fray if you have a strong opinion of your own and feel that you can convince your opponent? It's good mental exercise, it's a much more intelligent pastime than television or canasta, and there's always the chance that you'll win.

If you do, you'll feel a pleasant glow of satisfaction.

And if you lose, you'll have discovered your hidden bias, added to your mental flexibility, looked at things from another point of view, learned something you didn't know before, and gained some new understanding.

CHAPTER 11

Legal Rules and Lively Cases

General propositions do not decide concrete cases.
—Oliver Wendell Holmes

A month or so ago I was on jury duty. For two weeks I heard lawyers address each prospective juror with the time-honored question: "Are you going to take the law neither from me nor from my adversary but only from the judge?" And for two weeks I heard jurors solemnly pledge that they would.

Whereupon the jurors were duly selected, swore their oaths, listened to the lawyers' arguments, listened to the testimony, listened to the judge's charge, and went to the jury room to consider the verdict.

They did exactly what they had pledged to do, and took the law only from the judge.

And then, in most cases, they didn't apply it.

What do I mean by this? Am I accusing all juries of stupidity or willful malice? Not at all. Let me explain.

When you, as a layman, think of the law, the application of a legal rule to a specific case looks like a simple matter. Once you know what the law is—or once the judge has explained it to you if you sit on a jury —all you have to do is make sure of the facts. When you *have* the facts— or when the jury has agreed on them—you apply the rule, and your verdict follows almost automatically. You may have your doubts about the application of abstract rules to concrete situations in other fields; but not in law. That's what the law is, isn't it?—a body of rules and a procedure for applying the rules to cases.

Or so you think. But lawyers know better. "The assumption," one of them writes, "that the application of a law is merely . . . matching the rule against the case . . . is naïve and misleading."

Another lawyer, in a well-known book on legal reasoning, is even more explicit. "It cannot be said," he writes, "that the legal process is the application of known rules to diverse facts. . . . The rules change as the rules are applied." He then goes on to explain what happens in the application of case law, statutory law and the Constitution. Case law is applied by "classifying things as equal when they are somewhat different, justifying the classification by rules made up as the reasoning or classification proceeds." As to statutory law, "it is only folklore which holds that a statute if clearly written can be completely unambiguous and applied as intended to a specific case." And the Constitution? "The Constitution permits the court to be inconsistent."

Are you outraged? Does this offend your sense of justice? Wait a minute before you answer yes.

For one thing, you have to realize that justice doesn't necessarily mean the application of laws. That idea is just part of your upbringing in our Western civilization. The Chinese, for instance, whose civilization is a good deal older than ours, have a different notion. Confucius said he was for government by wise and just men and *against* government by laws. So, in traditional Chinese law, it's considered an *injustice* to base a decision on a general rule; the only fair thing, from the Chinese point of view, is to decide each individual case strictly on its own merits.

When it comes down to it, you are not as far removed from the Chinese point of view as you think you are. You don't *really* think that the law should be applied in each case. You see no harm in settling a case out of court, in compromising, in submitting to mediation or arbitration. You don't consider it an injustice if a policeman lets you off without a ticket. You are a concrete Chinese thinker in practice, but an abstract Western thinker in theory.

Even in theory, however, your faith in the application of rules to cases is hard to justify. There's the awkward fact that there seem to be *two* possible rules applying to each case, depending on which side you're on. And higher courts, ever so often, apply different rules from lower ones. And judges on the same bench have a habit of dissenting in their opinions. In fact, if a case comes to court at all, there is always some doubt as to what rule applies.

Here are, at random, a few cases I picked from the newspapers during the last year. Each could have been plausibly decided either way. Each is a slap in the face of the theory that the law means applying rules to cases.

Item: The C. F. Mueller Company made—and still makes—macaroni; all the money it made went to the New York University School of Law. So, the company said, it was a "corporation organized exclusively for educational purposes" and didn't have to pay income tax. The Internal Revenue Bureau said it had to pay taxes just like everybody else, since the macaroni business isn't education regardless of who gets the profits. The Tax Court sided with the Revenue Bureau. Maybe by the time you read this, the Supreme Court will have said the opposite.

Item: Irma Smith was employed by her father. According to the books, she drew a salary of $15,000, and that's what she paid income tax on. Then the government went over the company's books, thought $15,000 was too much, and decided that what Mr. Smith really paid his daughter was $9,000 at most. So Miss Smith asked for a refund of her personal income tax on the difference of $6,000. The Revenue Bureau said no; the change on the company's books had nothing to do with Miss Smith's personal taxes. In this case the Revenue Bureau lost. The U.S. District Court of New Jersey turned them down. (But just before this book went to press, a higher court decided the case the other way. See what I mean?)

Item: Another businessman, Mr. Bernard Glagovsky, also had a daughter. When Miss Glagovsky got married, her father thought he'd invite his customers and business acquaintances to the wedding. All in all, there were 350 guests and the bill was $9,200. Mr. Glagovsky felt that about 60 per cent of the amount was strictly a business expense and therefore deductible on his tax return. The Revenue Bureau, as always, disagreed. If Mr. Glagovsky liked to have two hundred customers and prospects join the celebrations, that was his own affair. The Tax Court felt the same way.

Item: Thomas Petro was born in Oklahoma in 1900. When he was ten, his parents moved to Canada. Petro senior became a naturalized Canadian. Automatically, Thomas became a Canadian citizen too. He grew up as a Canadian and voted in five Canadian elections. Then, in 1942, he went back to the United States, claiming he was still an American. The case came to court, and the court said he had to go back to Canada: a 1941 law said anyone voting in a foreign election lost his American citizenship. Whereupon Petro appealed to the U.S. Court of

Appeals and won: the higher court looked at the *same* 1941 law and discovered another provision in it that made him an American. It said that if you lose your U.S. citizenship because your parents were naturalized abroad, you get it back as soon as you return.

All of which should effectively cure you of the notion that you can apply a legal rule to a case and that's that. Trouble is, there are always at least *two* rules.

But then, where do the rules come from? In the bulk of our law, they are derived from previous decisions in similar cases. And since no two cases are ever exactly alike, this means that in case law, strictly speaking, there *are* no rules.

The law books are full of illustrations to prove this point. The most famous is the story of the so-called "inherently dangerous" rule. This deals with the question of whether the manufacturer of an article has to pay damages if the article injures someone who bought it from a retailer. The rule used to be that he was liable if the article was "inherently dangerous"—like a loaded gun—and wasn't if it was not. The distinction was first made in an English case in 1851 when a housewife was hurt by an exploding oil lamp; the court said then a lamp wasn't like a loaded gun and the manufacturer wasn't responsible.

In the horse-and-buggy days, of course, there was no trouble in applying this rule to vehicles: carriages, just like a lamp, were not "inherently dangerous." But then the automobile came in and things began to look different. The old rule didn't fit the times any more. So what happened? Very simple: The courts suddenly discovered there wasn't any such rule after all.

Before that discovery, in 1915, a Mr. Johnson bought a Cadillac whose wheel broke, and sued the Cadillac company for damages. He didn't get a penny because, as the court said,

. . . one who manufactures articles dangerous only if defectively made, or installed, e.g., tables, chairs, pictures or mirrors hung on the walls, carriages, automobiles, and so on is not liable to third parties for injuries caused by them, except in cases of willful injury or fraud.

A year later, in 1916, a Mr. MacPherson bought a Buick whose wheel broke, and sued the Buick company for damages. Mr. MacPherson was luckier than Mr. Johnson. Somehow, between 1915 and 1916, the old rule had melted away and Judge Benjamin Cardozo found that the Buick Motor Company had to pay.

The defendant argues, [he wrote] that things inherently dangerous to life are poisons, explosives, deadly weapons, things whose normal function is to injure or destroy. But whatever the rule may once have been . . . it has no longer that restricted meaning. . . . If the nature of a thing is such that it is reasonably certain to place life and limb in peril, when negligently made, it is then a thing of danger.

And with these words of Cardozo, the old rule vanished forever.

This famous example shows what can happen in case law, where rules are derived from court decisions. Surely, you'll say, things are different in statutory law, where rules are spelled out in so many words by legislators. But are they? Take the Displaced Persons Act of 1948. That law said the 40 per cent of all DP's must come from "de facto annexed countries and areas," meaning Estonia, Latvia and Lithuania. It turned out that this made it practically impossible to fill the annual quota of 205,000. So a year later the State Department discovered that "de facto annexed countries and areas" meant not only those three Baltic states, but also all territories administered by Russia or Poland under the Potsdam Agreement of 1945.

Usually, when there is a question about the meaning of an act of Congress, the lawyers say that you have to find the intent of the legislature. But that's a fiction. What it really means is that statutes are changed by suddenly declaring that Congress meant something different from what everybody thought it meant. This is easy because doubtful cases are exactly those that Congress either didn't foresee or deliberately left up in the air. For instance, in the recent revision of the minimum wage law, the law was narrowed to cover fewer workers. This is the way it was done. Congress can make laws only in connection with goods produced for interstate commerce; so the original law had referred to workers "necessary to" the production of goods for interstate commerce. The House of Representatives felt that these words had been interpreted too broadly by the Wage and Hour Administration and proposed to replace them by "indispensable to." The Senate wanted to stick to the old phrase "necessary to." Finally the House and the Senate compromised and settled on "workers engaged in a closely related process or occupation *directly essential to*" the production of goods for interstate commerce.

Now what does this mean when it comes to deciding a specific case? Does it mean that a man washing the windows of a firm engaged in interstate commerce has to be paid at least 75¢ an hour? Nobody knows. What was the intent of the legislature? Well, the congressmen who were for "indispensable to" obviously didn't mean to include the window-washer; those who wanted to stick to "necessary to" probably did. And those who finally voted for the compromise? Sometime in the future a judge will decide they meant one thing or the other.

That judge will do well to look at the circumstances of the case rather than search for what was in the minds of the congressmen who debated the bill. Otherwise he'll get confused by exchanges like this in the House:

> *Mr. Lucas:* . . . substituting the word "indispensable" for the word "necessary." These changes are needed in order to stem, and in some cases, reverse the action of the administrator and the courts in bringing under the act many businesses of a purely local type by giving to the word "necessary" an all-inclusive construction. . . .
>
> *Mr. Dondero:* Mr. Chairman, will the gentleman yield?
>
> *Mr. Lucas:* I yield to the gentleman from Michigan.
>
> *Mr. Dondero:* . . . What does the gentleman do in this bill in regard to caddies on golf courses, boys and girls who are in high school or now out of school during their vacations working and earning a little money picking fruit or picking vegetables, pulling weeds, and things of that kind? What does the gentleman do with them?
>
> *Mr. Lucas:* Well, sir, it is going to be difficult to find them in interstate commerce, but I do not question the ability of the administrator, the present administrator, to find that caddies are in interstate commerce, if they are handling golf balls which were produced across the State line, or if they are carrying golf clubs which are produced in another State, or if they are working for a traveling man. The administrator may well find them in interstate commerce.
>
> *Mr. Jacobs:* Mr. Chairman, will the gentleman yield?
>
> *Mr. Lucas:* I yield to the gentleman from Indiana.
>
> *Mr. Jacobs:* Has the administrator held caddies to be in interstate commerce?
>
> *Mr. Lucas:* I will answer the gentleman by saying that if he has not done so, it is because the problem has not yet been presented to him.

Does this sort of thing help in deciding a case by ascertaining the intent of the legislature? It does not. No wonder Senator Elbert D. Thomas came out of the House-Senate Conference telling reporters that the new law was an invitation to litigation. It might be ten or twelve years, he said, before the courts would interpret the meaning of *directly essential.*

So the rules of statutory law are just as open to shifts and changes as the rules of case law. There is even a famous case where a statute said one thing and a court said exactly the opposite. In 1885 Congress passed a law forbidding "the importation of foreigners . . . under contract . . . to perform labor in the United States." A few years later, Trinity Church in New York picked an English minister as its new pastor. A contract was signed, and the minister came to the United States. Whereupon the government sued the church for breaking the law. The Supreme Court pondered, found that the law applied to the case—and decided in favor of the church. Otherwise the result would be absurd, the court quietly explained.

The Trinity Church case is mentioned in the book *Courts on Trial* by Jerome Frank, in connection with Judge Frank's theory of legal interpretation. The courts interpret the law, Frank says, the way a musical performer interprets a composition. Until it is performed, a composition exists only on paper; it is the performer's vision and imagination that brings it to life. The law, too, is only a dead letter until a court interprets it in the light of an actual case.

For the ordinary layman, even this elegant analogy doesn't go far enough. What he wants is fairness and justice, and if the law doesn't seem fair and just, then he is all for playing by ear. The layman's legal heroes are not the master interpreters of the law. His heroes are Erle Stanley Gardner's Perry Mason and Arthur Train's Ephraim Tutt, who do right by their clients and let the niceties of the law go hang.

And this brings us back to the question of what happens to the law when it is put in the hands of laymen—the question of how a jury decides a case. You'll agree now, I hope, that they don't just apply the law to the facts of the case. But what do they do instead? What actually does happen in a jury room?

Well, in a case I sat on last month, a housewife sued a storekeeper because she had been injured by a defective piece of merchandise. The storekeeper swore she had never been in his store. The woman swore she had bought the article from him. The jury had to decide which one to believe.

It so happened that nine of us believed the woman and three the storekeeper. By the strict rules of law, that meant a hung jury and a new trial. Actually, it didn't mean any such thing. We compromised and awarded the woman a fraction of what she had asked for.

Typical? I think so. Not long ago a magazine writer described *her* experiences in a jury room. It was an automobile accident case. A boy riding a bicycle had been injured by a car after he had darted from a side road onto a busy highway. The law calls this "contributory negligence" and legally the boy wasn't entitled to a thing. But three jurors disagreed. One thought the driver had been speeding; one remembered a case in California where the driver had to pay $10,000; and a woman insisted that "that poor woman ought to have enough to send her boy to college." The jury tried to compromise but couldn't agree because the magazine writer was the only one who stuck to the letter of the law.

That experience was even more typical than my own. According to a statement by an experienced judge, Mr. Joseph N. Ulman, juries *always* disregard the law of contributory negligence. And, Judge Ulman adds, that's not at all unreasonable: the "illegal" law that the juries apply on the highways has always been the accepted law for accidents on the high seas.

Many people have come to the conclusion that juries are a good thing just *because* they often don't apply the law. James Gould Cozzens, in his novel *The Just and the Unjust*, has stated the case beautifully. In that novel, two men are on trial for murder because they have admittedly taken part in a kidnaping in which a man was killed. The actual murder was committed by a third man who is not on trial in that court. The judge explains to the jury that they can either find the two men guilty of first-degree murder (for participating in the kidnaping that led to murder) or else acquit them. The jury, however, disregards the law and returns a verdict of second-degree murder, saving the two men from execution. As one of the characters remarks, "The jury was jibing at executing two men for something they argued a third man had really done."

To which old Judge Coates (the author's spokesman) replies:

"A jury has its uses. That's one of them. It's like a cylinder head gasket. Between two things that don't give any, you have to have something that does give a little, something to seal the law to the facts. There isn't any known way to legislate with an allowance for right feeling. . . . The jury protects the court. It's a question how long any system of courts could last in a free country if judges found the verdicts. It doesn't matter how wise and experienced the judges may be. Resentment would build up every time the findings didn't go with current notions or prejudices. Pretty soon half the community would want to lynch the judge. There's no focal point with a jury; the jury is the public itself. That's why a jury can say when a judge couldn't, 'I don't care what the law is, that isn't right and I won't do it.' It's the greatest prerogative of free men."

He might have added that it's also the greatest prerogative of *intelligent* men: to rise above the abstract rules of law, formal logic, or mere convention, and meet each new problem on its own terms.

CHAPTER 12

Enter a Bright Idea

They showed characteristic insight behavior and were disgusted with failure to see the solution earlier.

—Norman R. F. Maier, *Reasoning in Humans*

Let me tell you the story of a bright idea.

In 1949 a Congressional fight broke out over federal aid to education. The debate didn't center on the principle of aid to public schools, but on the question of whether private schools should get it too. Catholic congressmen, thinking of their parochial schools, felt they should—not for religious instruction, to be sure, but for collateral services such as health, transportation and nonreligious books. Other congressmen insisted that, as a matter of principle, private schools should get no federal money whatever.

The debate went on for weeks and months. Neither side was willing to give an inch. Legislation was stalled.

At this point, Senator Paul H. Douglas of Illinois hit upon an idea. He described it later in a magazine article:

Whether children are in public or private schools, and whether they are Protestant, Catholic or Jewish, children present a uniform health problem, and what is done to improve their health has a beneficial effect upon the community as a whole. In consequence, it appeared to me that a distinction could be drawn between health services on the one hand and transportation and books on the other; that federal aid for these health services should be furnished to all children, whether they were in private or public schools. Under this view, the schoolhouse at certain hours in the term would have the status of a convenient neighborhood dispensary.

Senator Douglas drafted a bill along these lines, which was promptly approved by the proper Senate Committee. The debate went on in the House, however; as I am writing, the issue is still unresolved.

But this doesn't concern me right now. What interests me is that we have here a simon-pure, test-tube specimen of what is usually called a bright idea. It has all the earmarks: a seemingly insoluble problem, a neat, simple solution, and that feeling of "Why, that's it, of course! Why didn't *I* think of that!"

If there is any secret of clear thinking, this is it. What is the nature of a bright idea? How do you get one? Where does it come from?

Ask anybody these questions, and the answer is apt to be: "A bright idea comes to you out of nowhere in a flash of inspiration."

Very simple. Very unsatisfactory, too. Doesn't tell you a thing.

Do psychologists have a better answer? They do, in a way. Their answer is far from simple, and not quite satisfactory either. But it's fascinating and well worth knowing.

To understand what the psychologists are talking about, let's go back to the chimpanzees we met in the first chapter. Psychologists don't study bright ideas, they study "problem-solving"; and they like to strip things down to essentials. To them, a senator wrestling with a knotty problem in legislation is essentially the same thing as a chimpanzee trying to get at some bananas that are out of reach. Both are examples of problem-solving behavior; one situation is a thousand times more complex than the other, but basically there's no difference.

The first step in problem-solving is a thorough study of the problem situation. The chimpanzee looks through the bars of his cage at the bananas, sees that he can't reach them, surveys the inside of the cage, focuses on all the objects inside—including the stick—and ponders. The senator looks at federal aid to education, sees that a compromise seems impossible, surveys Catholic and non-Catholic reasoning, focuses on schools, children, teachers, buildings and collateral services—including health—and ponders. Both consider all the elements in the situation before they are ready to solve the problem.

Next come two steps. They are taken simultaneously or one after the other.

One is an effort to find the factor that can be moved or changed. If that factor were obvious, there'd be no problem but a routine operation. (If you want to ring a bell, you push the button.) A problem arises whenever the key factor is hidden; you don't see it because it looks like an inconspicuous bit of background. The stick is one of many things inside the cage; it *looks* like just another object that happens to be around. Health services are lumped together with transportation and books under the heading "collateral services"; they *look* like just another minor part of school expenditures. To solve the problem, you have to focus on the key factor and mentally "pry it loose." You have to see the stick as something that can be pushed through bars; you have to realize that health services may serve as a basis for a compromise.

The other step is not a survey of the situation before you, but a survey of your mind. You search among your memories for a pattern that would fit the situation. Again, if that pattern were obvious, there'd be no problem. You have to find a pattern that is usually *not* applied to this sort of problem. The chimpanzee thinks of games he played and remembers how he used a stick to "make a long arm"; the senator thinks of community services and remembers health centers and dispensaries. Is there a parallel? Does that mental framework fit the situation? Would it change it so that the problem can be solved?

As I said, the two steps may come at the same time. One psychologist, Dr. Duncker, calls them the approach "from below" and the approach "from above." Basically, they are two ways of doing the same thing: you try to look at the situation in a different light.

And then—after you have pried loose a key factor or found a new pattern—something clicks and the bright idea appears. It isn't a flash of inspiration, psychologists insist. It's what happens in your brain when a remembered pattern matches the pattern of the situation before you. If you want a picturesque phrase, the best psychologists have to offer is the word *Aha!-experience.*

So there you are. Disappointed? Did you expect a magic formula, a big wonderful secret? If so, I'm sorry; psychology doesn't seem to work that way. It'll be a long time until psychologists can produce miracles.

Meanwhile, I think their researches in problem-solving are highly valuable. If you want to know how to get bright ideas, by far the best thing is to look closely at their experiments and illustrations. Let me describe two, one showing a solution "from below," the other a solution "from above."

The first is one of Dr. Duncker's ingenious experiments. It's one of a series in which he asked people to solve simple mechanical problems.

Here is the situation: You are led into a room with a table in it. You are told that the room is to be used for visual experiments and you're supposed to put three small candles side by side on the door, at eye level. On the table there are all sorts of materials for you to work with: paper clips, paper, string, pencils, tinfoil, ash trays, and so on. There are also three little cardboard boxes; the first contains a few short, thin candles, the second contains tacks, and the third contains matches. How are you going to put up the candles? (If you want to, put the book down at this point and try to figure out the answer.)

Stumped? If you are like Dr. Duncker's test subjects, you probably are. Only 43 per cent of them solved the problem. Fifty-seven per cent looked at the door and the candles, spent two or three minutes picking up this or that object from the table, and then gave up. They couldn't think of a possible way of getting those candles up on the door.

The solution is very simple once you know it. You empty the three boxes and tack them onto the door as platforms for the candles.

Now why is this so difficult to think of? The answer is clear: the three boxes are "fixed" in the problem situation; to solve the problem, you have to "pry them loose." Dr. Duncker proved this neatly by slight changes in the experimental setup. First he repeated the experiment, but left the boxes empty. Result: The problem was solved by *all* subjects. Then he filled the boxes not with candles, tacks, and matches, but with buttons—that is, he pushed the key factor even farther into the background. Result: The percentage of those who *failed* rose from 57 per cent to 86 per cent.

The ability to solve problems this way is the ability to spot things that are hard to distinguish from their background. Psychologists have devised several tests to measure this ability; one of them, the "Gottschaldt Figures Test," is referred to in Dr. Duncker's work. You will find it on pages 94 to 98.

I can see you looking at these little geometrical designs and wondering. Seems like a children's game, you say. Is there really a connection between these figures and the art of thinking?

There certainly is, and I can prove it. During World War II, Dr. L. L. Thurstone of the University of Chicago gave a group of Washington administrators a battery of seventy tests to find out what mental abilities are most important for executives. He worked out the statistical relationship between these tests on the one hand and salaries and ratings for professional promise on the other. *Of all seventy tests, the one most closely related to administrative success was the Gottschaldt Figures Test.* Which seems to mean that an executive is essentially a problem-solver, and problem-solving means being able to spot the key factor in a confusing situation.

PART I

In each pair of figures below, mark that part of the
second figure which is the same as the first.

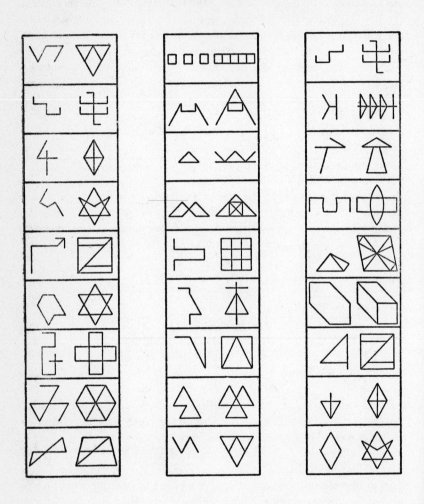

PART II

Look at the adjacent figure.

It is contained in each of the
drawings below. Find it in each
drawing and then mark it. Mark
only one figure in each drawing.

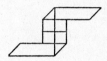 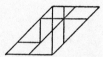 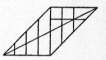

 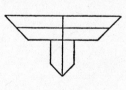 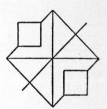

Look at the two adjacent figures. One of them
is contained in each of the drawings below.

In each of the following drawings, mark that part
which is the same as one of the adjacent figures.
Mark only one figure in each drawing.

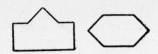

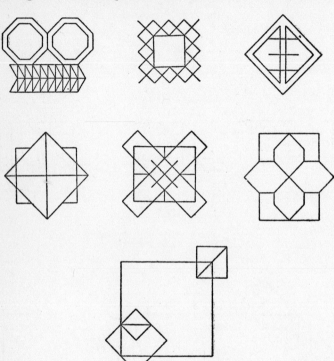

PART IV

Look at the two adjacent figures.
One of them is contained in each of
the drawings below.

In each of the following drawings, mark
that part which is the same as one of the
adjacent figures. Mark only one figure
in each drawing.

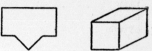

PART V

Look at the two adjacent figures.
One of them is contained in each
of the drawings below.

In each of the following drawings,
mark that part which is the same
as one of the adjacent figures.
Mark only one figure in each
drawing.

 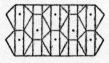 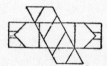

 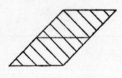 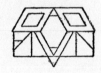

98

If you want to take this test, all you need to do is take a pencil and trace each of the "hidden figures." Before you start each page, look at your watch. Part I on page 94 is easier than the rest; an average person takes about five minutes to mark all twenty-seven figures. Parts II to V on pages 95 to 98 are more difficult; an average person takes about fifteen minutes to do all thirty-four figures. (If you're a whiz, you may be able to do page 94 in two minutes and pages 95 to 98 in six.)

And now let's look at another example of problem-solving—this time a solution "from above," through using a different mental framework. I take this illustration from *Productive Thinking*, the brilliant book by the late Dr. Max Wertheimer. The example is not as ingenious as Dr. Duncker's box problem, but far more illuminating.

Dr. Wertheimer tells how he was looking out the window one day and saw two boys playing badminton in the garden. (He calls the boys A and B, but I'll call them Andy and Bill.) Andy was twelve, Bill was only ten. They played several sets, but Bill was a much poorer player and lost all the games.

Dr. Wertheimer watched and listened. Bill got more and more unhappy. He had no chance at all. Andy often served him so cleverly that he couldn't possibly return the bird. Finally Bill threw down his racket, sat on a tree trunk and said: "I won't play any more." Andy tried to talk him out of it, but Bill didn't answer. Then Andy sat down too. Both boys looked unhappy. They were faced with what seemed an insoluble problem.

What would *you* have done in Andy's place? Dr. Wertheimer says he asked many people the same question, but hardly anybody arrived at Andy's intelligent solution. What actually happened was this:

At first, Andy was simply angry. "Why don't you go ahead?" he asked Bill. "Why do you break up the game? Do you think it's nice to stop in this silly way?"

There was a pause. Andy glanced at Bill, and Bill just looked sad. Then Andy said in a different tone of voice: "I'm sorry."

There was another pause. Suddenly Andy said: "Look here. Such playing *is* nonsense." He looked as if something slowly began to dawn on him, and continued: "This sort of game is funny. I'm not really unfriendly to you. . . ." And then he mumbled something like "Must it . . . ?" His face lit up and he said happily: "I have an idea—let's play this way: Let's see how long we can keep the bird going between us and count how many times it goes back and forth without falling. What score could we make? Do you think we could make it ten or twenty? We'll start with easy serves but then let's make them harder and harder . . ."

Bill agreed happily: "That's a good idea. Let's."

They started to play—not the competitive game of badminton, but a different, co-operative new game. Andy had solved the problem.

There's a long analysis of this example in Dr. Wertheimer's book, and I wish I could quote it all. He points out that Andy solved the problem by completely changing his mental picture of the situation. Instead of looking at the game as something that existed for his own enjoyment and at Bill as someone to play against, he suddenly saw the game as something to be enjoyed by both of them. "Often," Wertheimer writes, "one must first forget what he happens to wish before he can become susceptible to what the situation itself requires. . . . This transition is one of the great moments in many genuine thought processes. . . . Real thinkers forget about themselves in thinking."

Not only that, real thinkers can detach their minds from habitual, established patterns of thought and apply far removed, seemingly unrelated mental frameworks. Their mind doesn't move in narrow grooves but ranges over a wide area of possible patterns.

The newspapers, not long ago, carried a report of brain wave studies on Albert Einstein and a couple of other mathematical geniuses. The theory behind the experiments was that a creative, original thinker has the ability to quickly "scan" one group of brain cells after another. It was found that Einstein's brain did this much better and faster than an ordinary brain.

All of which gives you a pretty clear picture of how you can get bright ideas. After studying a problem, do either or both of these things:

1. Look for a seemingly irrelevant key factor in the situation.
2. Look for a seemingly unsuitable pattern in your mind.

This isn't very specific, but it's obviously more helpful than just sitting and waiting for an inspiration.

Let me wind up this chapter with a bright idea that made history. With Duncker's and Wertheimer's studies in mind, read how Franklin D. Roosevelt thought up the idea of Lend-Lease.

In December, 1940, Britain desperately needed material help against the Nazis. The United States, however, was not at war; Congress and the people were unwilling to give Britain a tremendous loan to buy war materials. How to help Britain without a loan was a seemingly insoluble problem.

On December 2, Roosevelt went on a two-weeks' Caribbean cruise. He spent those two weeks in thinking over the problem, searching for the key factor, the novel pattern.

After two weeks he returned. He had solved the "impossible" problem. He called a press conference and explained his simple plan to help Britain: "Now, what I am trying to do is eliminate the dollar sign. That is something brand-new in the thoughts of everybody in this room, I think—get rid of the silly, foolish old dollar sign. . . . Well, let me give you an illustration. Suppose my neighbor's home catches fire, and I have a length of garden hose . . ."

You see the two basic ingredients of a bright idea? Roosevelt had found the "detachable" key factor—the dollar sign; and he had found a totally new pattern no one had ever thought of in connection with a foreign loan—lending your neighbor a garden hose.

It was brilliantly simple. And it changed the course of history.

CHAPTER 13

How to Solve a Puzzle

Experience has shown, and a true philosophy will always show, that a vast, perhaps the larger, portion of the truth arises from the seemingly irrelevant.

—Edgar Allan Poe, "The Mystery of Marie Rogêt"

A good many years ago Mr. A. A. Milne—who gave our children the Winnie-the-Pooh books—wrote a column for a British magazine. He faithfully produced a charming little essay for every issue until he suddenly found himself stymied. As he explained to his readers the next time, someone had challenged him with a word game and he was unable to think of anything else until he had solved it. The word—whose rearranged letters spell an everyday English word—was

TERALBAY.

According to legend, Lord Melbourne gave this word to Queen Victoria once and it kept her awake all night.

Mr. Milne didn't tell his readers what the solution was. But he explained clearly his *method* of solution.

The way to solve a problem of this sort is to waggle your eyes and see what you get. If you do this, words like *alterably* and *laboratory* emerge, which a little thought shows you to be wrong. You may then waggle your eyes again, look at it upside down or sideways, or stalk it carefully from the southwest and plunge upon it suddenly when it is not ready for you. . . . I have no doubt that after hours of immense labor you will triumphantly suggest *rateably*. I suggested that myself, but it is wrong. There is no such word in the dictionary. The same objection applies to *bat-early*—it ought to mean something, but it doesn't.

I don't mean to say that the Milne Method of solving word games is bad. It's more or less what everybody does, and it's basically sound. But it can be improved upon.

The *teralbay* kind of puzzle—like every other kind—has a hidden clue somewhere. Once you've spotted it, the puzzle is solved. The difficulty lies in the fact that the situation before you is confused; you have to get rid of the confusion before you can even start working on the problem. After all, the point is not to read the word *teralbay* over and over to find a hidden meaning, but to form a new word from the letters *t, e, r, a, l, b, a* and *y*.

So the thing to do is this: Try at random other patterns of arrangement, in the hope that the hidden clue will emerge in the process. You may arrange the letters alphabetically

A A B E L R T Y

or in reversed alphabetical order

Y T R L E B A A

or alphabetically with alternating consonants and vowels

B A L A R E T Y

or the same reversed

Y T E R A L A B

and so on. Or you may try arrangements ending in *able* or *ably* like

R A Y T A B L E

or

T E A R A B L Y .

(This last one you'll find in small type in Webster's Unabridged, but it obviously won't do.)

If you do this—systematically run through various random arrangements—you'll have a better chance than if you just waggle your eyes. At least, I used that method and finally did solve the puzzle, after hours of work. When I got to the *able* words, I happened upon

T R A Y A B L E .

I liked that word very much, but in the end I had to admit that there wasn't any such word. However, the *tray* in it turned out to be the hidden clue: suddenly I had the solution. Of course! What Lord Melbourne meant was— (You may want to play with this, so I put the solution on page 196, along with solutions to the other puzzles in this chapter.)

In other words, the first step in getting rid of confusion is rearrangement. Any kind of rearrangement is better than staring at the confusing arrangement before you. For example, there's the sign a GI saw on a post in Italy during World War II:

TOTI
EMUL
ESTO

String the letters out in one line instead of three, and you'll have no trouble.

Often, however, rearrangement is not enough. You have to do some sort of translation; you have to look at the elements in the puzzle in some other form. Eugenio Rignano, in his *Psychology of Reasoning*, has a fine example of this. He was surprised and puzzled, he writes, when he heard for the first time this sentence: "Since more people live in London than anyone has hairs on his head, there must be at least two people there with the same number of hairs." Yet he immediately realized that this was so when he began mentally to line up the inhabitants of London, starting with a totally bald man, followed by a man with one hair, a man with two hairs, and so on. Naturally, since the population of London is larger than the maximum number of hairs on people's heads, he had lots of leftover people whose hair-count matched that of people in the lineup. Visualized in this way, the puzzle was no puzzle any more.

Another kind of translation is the use of mathematical symbols. It's the best technique, for instance, if you want to solve the following type of puzzle:

The ages of a man and his wife are together 98. He is twice as old as she was when he was the age she is today. What are their ages?

This is easy to solve if you know enough algebra to set up a couple of equations, calling, say, the husband's age x and the wife's age y.

Maybe you have the feeling that the puzzles I have given you so far are particularly mean. You are right. They are problems plus: puzzles with an extra element of confusion added. Let's now look at some problems that are presented straight.

Here's a nice example. Read the following sentence and count how many *f*'s there are:

> Finished files are the results of years of scientific study combined with the experiences of years.

(Now do it again slowly and see if you were right the first time.)

Then there are two neat problems that I gave dozens of my friends and students last year.

1. Find the smallest number that can be divided evenly by 7 but leaves a remainder of 1 when divided by 2, 3, 4, 5, or 6.

2. Smith, Brown, Jones, and Robinson played three rubbers of bridge at 1¢ a point. No one had the same partner twice. Playing against Jones, Brown won a rubber of 900 points. Smith won a 600-point rubber, the smallest of the evening, when he played against Robinson. Jones lost $10 altogether. How did Robinson fare?

I ought to warn you that it may take you quite a while to solve these two problems. My friends and students took anywhere from five minutes to an hour for each. (There was an interesting difference in their way of going about it; I'll come to that in Chapter 17.) But—since I want to make a point here—I'll give you a break: the key to the solution in both cases is the seemingly irrelevant word *smallest*. In the first puzzle you have to find the *smallest* number, in the second you are told that the 600-point rubber was the *smallest* of the evening. Among my human guinea pigs 24 per cent overlooked that clue in the first puzzle and 32 per cent in the second.

These figures may seem incredible. Why should a bunch of intelligent adults have trouble spotting these simple clues? Why should one-fourth or one-third of them overlook these clues, with all the time in the world to solve the problem? Once you know it, the word *smallest* in both puzzles seems to stick out like a sore thumb. How is it possible not to see it?

This is the sort of question you ask yourself after you have finished a good mystery story. "Why, of course!" you say to yourself. "X was the murderer; I ought to have guessed that long ago. The clues were all there, right in front of my nose. How did I manage to miss them?"

The basic principle, then, of most puzzles or mystery stories is the "hidden" clue—the thing that you don't see because it seems utterly irrelevant. The question is: Is this only a feature of made-up puzzles and mysteries or does the principle operate in real-life problems too?

It so happens that the two most famous authors of mystery stories provided an answer to this question—Edgar Allan Poe and Sir Arthur Conan Doyle. Both ventured into the detection of actual crimes; both were highly successful. Let's see how the methods of C. Auguste Dupin and Sherlock Holmes apply to real-life mysteries.

Poe turned detective when he cleared up the case of Mary Cecilia Rogers, who was murdered near New York City in 1842. He chose to publish his solution, thinly disguised as fiction, in the story "The Mystery of Marie Rogêt." It is a matter of history that Poe's solution was essentially right and that of the police was wrong.

Mary Rogers lived with her mother on Nassau Street and was employed in a cigar store downtown. One Sunday morning in June she left home (supposedly to visit an aunt) and disappeared. Four days later her body was found in the Hudson near Weehawken. The official theory was that she had been the victim of a gang of hoodlums.

Poe knew nothing about the case except what he had read in the papers. But by analyzing the published facts he disproved the theory that the murder was the work of a gang and showed who the real murderer was.

We don't need to go into all the details here, since Poe's main point was very simple. Mary Rogers had disappeared once before, about three-and-a-half years before her death; at that time she had turned up again after a week, behaving as if nothing had happened. Obviously she had spent that week with a lover. Neither the police nor the newspapers connected that earlier disappearance with her tragic death three years later; they didn't see any parallel between an old amorous adventure and a kidnaping by a gang. Poe focused on that seemingly irrelevant clue; once he had done so, everything fell into place and it was clear that Mary Rogers was murdered by her lover.

Conan Doyle's performance as a real-life detective didn't deal with a murder, but the case was even more spectacular than that of Mary Rogers. There had been a flagrant miscarriage of justice.

In December, 1906, the creator of Sherlock Holmes received a letter and a batch of newspaper clippings from a man named George Edalji. Mr. Edalji had just been released from prison after having served three years for a crime of which he had been convicted. He was unable to continue his career as a lawyer and asked Conan Doyle to help him prove his innocence.

Conan Doyle—like Poe sixty-four years earlier—studied the newspaper clippings. He learned that Edalji had been declared guilty of killing animals near the village of Great Wyrley in 1903. The killings had obviously been the work of a maniac who roamed the countryside by night; they had been accompanied and announced by mad anonymous letters sent to the local police. The letters—together with other circumstantial evidence—convinced the police, and later the court, that Edalji was the killer. Their most damning feature was their similarity to a group of anonymous letters written seven years before. Those earlier letters had been directed against George Edalji's father and the police had always considered George their author.

Conan Doyle—again like Poe sixty-four years earlier—found the clue in the previous event. He too focused on a seemingly irrelevant point. These are his words:

At the beginning, one point is so obvious that I wonder it has escaped notice. This is the extraordinary long gap between the two sets of letters. Letters, childish hoaxes, abound up to late December of '95. Then, for nearly seven years, *nobody* gets an abusive letter. To me this did not suggest that the culprit had changed his whole character and habits overnight, reverting to them with equal malice in 1903. It suggested absence; that someone had been away during that time.

After this, the solution of the mystery was easy. All that was necessary was to find someone in the community who had spent those seven years abroad or at sea and fitted the description of a mad letter-writer and animal-killer. The man was found and, after a long struggle, George Edalji was publicly vindicated and readmitted to the bar.

Do these two cases prove my point? I think so. But, after all, you may say, Edgar Allan Poe and Sir Arthur Conan Doyle were amateur detectives. Do professional detectives work the same way in solving a puzzling case?

The newspapers recently carried a story that shows the essence of professional detective work. I mean the story of Mr. Goetz's Van Gogh.

In 1949 Mr. William Goetz, a Hollywood movie executive, bought a picture by Vincent Van Gogh called "Study by Candlelight." He paid over $50,000 for it. After some time Van Gogh's nephew, Mr. Vincent W. Van Gogh, declared publicly that the picture was a fake. Mr. Goetz didn't take this lying down and submitted the picture to a jury of experts appointed by the Metropolitan Museum in New York.

"Study by Candlelight" is a self-portrait of Van Gogh, resembling his many other self-portraits. It bears his signature, has a title in his handwriting, and includes a small study of a Japanese head and some Japanese inscriptions. The jury studied all this, together with the material, the colors, the brushwork and so on, and declared the painting as doubtful at best. "Any one of the unfavorable factors might be accounted for in reason," they concluded, "but the accumulation was too great to be counterbalanced; furthermore, the favorable factors were broad and intangible."

Mr. Goetz naturally wasn't happy with this verdict. He hit upon an ingenious plan. He shipped the picture back to Europe and then brought it back to the United States. There the expected thing happened: the Treasury Department asked for a $5,000 customs duty, since the picture was a fake and not a duty-free original work of art. Mr. Goetz refused to pay a penny since in *his* opinion it was a genuine Van Gogh. And so the case was thrown into the lap of professional Treasury Department detectives.

The detectives analyzed everything the jury of experts had analyzed before. But they focused on one thing the four art experts had paid no attention to whatever: the meaning of the Japanese inscriptions. Three Japanese experts were called in and promptly found some typical mistakes a European would make; what's more, they found those same mistakes in other Japanese inscriptions by Van Gogh whose authenticity was known.

Whereupon the Treasury Department decided that Mr. Goetz was the owner of a genuine Van Gogh.

Of course, it is still possible that the museum experts were right and the detectives were wrong. That's not my point. My point is that the professional detectives—just like those two illustrious amateurs, Poe and Conan Doyle—solved the case by focusing on a seemingly irrelevant detail. They found a "hidden" fact that had been in plain view all the time.

Probably this phrase will remind you of another of Edgar Allan Poe's classic tales—"The Purloined Letter." In that story, the police know that a certain blackmailer is in possession of a stolen letter; they repeatedly search him and his apartment but can't find it. Poe's detective genius, C. Auguste Dupin, figures that the clever criminal must have hidden the letter by putting it right under the noses of the police. So he pays a visit to the blackmailer in his room and immediately spots a half-torn, soiled, crumpled envelope in a "card-rack of pasteboard that hung dangling by a dirty blue ribbon from a little brass knob just beneath the middle of the mantelpiece."

Dupin explains the principle of his solution like this:

> There is a game of puzzles which is played upon a map. One party playing requires another to find a given word—the name of town, river, state, or empire—any word, in short, upon the motley and perplexed surface of the chart. A novice in the game generally seeks to embarrass his opponents by giving them the most minutely lettered names; but the adept selects such words as stretch, in large characters, from one end of the chart to the other. These, like the over-largely lettered signs and placards of the street, escape observation by dint of being excessively obvious; and here the physical oversight is precisely analogous with the moral inapprehension by which the intellect suffers to pass unnoticed those considerations which are too obtrusively and too palpably self-evident.

"The Purloined Letter" was not the first of Poe's classic detective stories but the third. Yet in a sense all mystery stories are variations upon its theme. There is good reason for that: A mystery writer who observes the established rules of the game must do two things: (*a*) he must show the detective-hero's ingenuity in solving the puzzle, and (*b*) he must play fair with the reader and give him a chance to solve the puzzle himself. He must therefore hide and reveal the important clues at the same time. The only way to do this is to mention them casually in the course of the story as if they were irrelevant. In other words, they must be hidden in plain view like "The Purloined Letter."

Recently a well-known mystery writer, giving away some of his trade secrets, made this point very clear:

> How does your detective find out who did it? He may no longer, as he could in Sherlock's time, pick up significant clues and pocket them, with neither by your leave nor explanation to the reader. He may not—at least not too obviously—rely on intuition. . . . And if he relies on the method of slow accumulation the reader will grow bored. . . . The modern answer, by and large, is the gimmick—the single, or perhaps double, revealing clue, *which the reader might also notice were he bright enough.*

So, if you want to train yourself in clear thinking and problem-solving, you might do worse than read whodunits—those perennial variations upon Poe's "The Purloined Letter" or, for that matter, upon Dr. Duncker's box problem. Mind you, you'll have to avoid the corpse-cluttered, hard-boiled pseudo mysteries, and you'll have to match your wits actively with the detective rather than passively wait for the solution. But if you read standard-formula whodunits in the proper spirit, they may well help you tackle your everyday problems.

Most of those problems, too, are solved by looking sharply at something that's been staring you in the face all the time.

C H A P T E R   1 4

Animal, Vegetable or Mineral

A classification is a repertory of weapons for attack upon the future and the unkown.

—John Dewey, *Reconstruction in Philosophy*

The birth of ideas has often been described. Poets talk of divine inspiration, ordinary people talk of hunches, psychologists talk of combinations, incubations, intimations and illuminations, Professor Wertheimer talks of recentering and restructuring, Professor Spearman talks of the educing of correlates, and the patent law talks of the flash of genius. Everybody seems to agree that ideas are born suddenly and mysteriously.

Well and good. Luckily we all have those hunches and flashes of insight and get our fair share of ideas after a good night's sleep, or while we are shaving, or during a hot bath.

But what if we don't? What if there is a problem to be solved and we have no clue, no routine to fall back on, and no happy inspiration? Is there a method by which we can hunt for ideas systematically, prosaically, in broad daylight?

There *is* such a method. As far as I know, it is the only one.

Thomas Hobbes, in 1651, described it this way:

Regulated thought is a seeking. Sometimes a man seeks what he has lost. . . . Sometimes a man knows a place determinate, within the compass whereof he is to seek; and then his thoughts run over all the parts thereof, in the same manner as one would sweep a room to find a jewel; or as a spaniel ranges the field, till he find a scent; or as a man should run over the alphabet, to start a rhyme.

A twentieth-century chemist, Dr. Wilder D. Bancroft, said the same thing in more modern terms:

. . . One must eventually present something constructive. The answer is to be found in the game of Twenty Questions. When I was a small boy, it was a very popular game to try to find, by asking a series of questions, what the others had selected. The first question was always: animal, vegetable or mineral? After that the questions must be ones that could be answered by yes or no. . . . The trick was to frame the questions so as to eliminate a large portion of the possible field each time and to reach the goal by successive eliminations. . . . The method might be called the either-or method, or the Socratic method. The latter sounds more impressive. That simple little game exemplifies the principles of scientific research and it would be a good thing if our graduate students would play it regularly as part of their research training.

Dr. Bancroft was right in comparing idea-hunting to the game of twenty questions, but he was quite wrong in calling this the Socratic method. Actually, the twenty questions game is exactly the opposite of the yes-or-no game the ancient Greeks used to play. In the yes-or-no game, the questioner started with his mind set on a certain answer and won by forcing his opponent to admit that foregone conclusion; in twenty questions, the questioner starts with a completely open mind and wins by forcing his opponent to reveal the answer. In the yes-or-no game the aim was to fight off ideas; in twenty questions the aim is to capture them.

And that's why, if you're interested in producing ideas, the Greek yes-or-no game is useless, while the game of twenty questions is the ideal model. It is well worth close study.

Let's spend a few minutes eavesdropping on twenty questions as it is played every week on the air. Our master of ceremonies is Bill Slater; the regulars are Fred Vandeventer, newscaster, Florence Rinard, his wife, Herb Polesie, movie producer, and young Johnny McPhee; the guest this particular evening is Miss Nina Foch, the actress.

Here is one game:

Bill Slater: This one's vegetable.
Mystery Voice: Here we go back to the days when knights were bold indeed. Bill is asking them to identify King Arthur's Round Table.
Bill Slater: Mystery Voice has told our friends at home. This is going to take a bit of a battle, I think.
Fred Vandeventer: Is it wood or a wood product?
Bill Slater: Yes.
Fred Vandeventer: Is it wood?

Bill Slater: It's wood.
Johnny McPhee: Does this thing exist?
Bill Slater: No.
Florence Rinard: If it did exist, would it be manufactured?
Bill Slater: Yes, if this did exist it would be manufactured.
Herb Polesie: Is it connected with one professional person?
Bill Slater: Yes.
Florence Rinard: Was it large enough for people to be inside of it?
Bill Slater: No. What were you thinking of?
Florence Rinard: A wooden horse.
Bill Slater: Yes, that's what you were thinking of—the Trojan Horse.
Florence Rinard: Is this in American fiction?
Bill Slater: No.
Fred Vandeventer: Is it in British fiction?
Bill Slater: Yes, partly there.
Fred Vandeventer: Is it in prose fiction?
Bill Slater: It has been in that form, yes.
Fred Vandeventer: Is it small enough to be carried about?
Bill Slater: No.
Florence Rinard: Is it a building?
Bill Slater: No, it's not a building.
Fred Vandeventer: Is it a means of transportation?
Bill Slater: No.
Fred Vandeventer: Is there any other—I'll ask this a different way: When this is manufactured, is it put together with something else?
Bill Slater: Well, usually yes.
Fred Vandeventer: I mean such as nails and screws and—
Bill Slater: Yes. The sort of thing you're after is usually put together with things like that.
Florence Rinard: Is this a piece of furniture?
Bill Slater: Yes.
Florence Rinard: Is it a chair?
Bill Slater: No.
Johnny McPhee: Is it a table?
Bill Slater: It's a table!
Johnny McPhee: A round table?
Bill Slater: Yes.
Johnny McPhee: King Arthur's Round Table?
Bill Slater: Right!

Another game:

Bill Slater: The subject's vegetable.
Mystery Voice: The state of Vermont is famous for a number of things. But when your sweet tooth is watering, you think of The Maple Trees of Vermont.
Fred Vandeventer: Is this wood or a wood product?

Bill Slater: Is it wood or a wood product? I have to say yes to that.

Johnny McPhee: Is it manufactured?

Bill Slater: No.

Johnny McPhee: Are we after a tree or part of a tree?

Bill Slater: Partly.

Johnny McPhee: A group of trees?

Bill Slater: A group of trees.

Johnny McPhee: Are they fictional?

Bill Slater: No, they're real.

Florence Rinard: Do they exist?

Bill Slater: They exist.

Florence Rinard: Are they in Europe?

Bill Slater: No, they're not in Europe.

Fred Vandeventer: Are they in the United States?

Bill Slater: They are in the United States.

Herb Polesie: Are they in California?

Bill Slater: They are not in California. You're thinking of the redwood trees.

Herb Polesie: Indeed, and beautiful they are.

Johnny McPhee: Are they east of the Mississippi?

Bill Slater: They are.

Johnny McPhee: And south of the Mason-Dixon line?

Bill Slater: No.

Fred Vandeventer: Are they—If you were approaching them from the south, would you cross the Hudson River to get to them?

Bill Slater: Yes, you would.

Fred Vandeventer: Are they in New England?

Bill Slater: Yes.

Florence Rinard: Are they one particular kind of trees?

Bill Slater: They are.

Florence Rinard: Maple?

Bill Slater: Yes.

Florence Rinard: Are they the trees they get maple syrup from?

Bill Slater: Yes.

Johnny McPhee: Any particular state?

Bill Slater: Yes.

Johnny McPhee: The maple sugar trees of Vermont?

Bill Slater: Right!

A third game:

Bill Slater: This subject is animal.

Mystery Voice: The subject this time is that fabled Face on the Barroom Floor.

Johnny McPhee: Is this a whole animal?

Bill Slater: No, this is not.

Florence Rinard: Is this a living animal?
Bill Slater: No, this is not a living animal.
Fred Vandeventer: Is it part of a human being?
Bill Slater: It's part of a human being you're after, yes.
Herb Polesie: Does my mother-in-law look like this in any way?
Bill Slater: I doubt it, Herb.
Johnny McPhee: Is this human being fictional?
Bill Slater: Yes, the human being involved is fictional.
Fred Vandeventer: Is this part of a man?
Bill Slater: No, it's not part of a man.
Florence Rinard: Is this in American fiction?
Bill Slater: Yes, I think you'd call it American fiction.
Fred Vandeventer: Is it in prose fiction?
Bill Slater: No.
Johnny McPhee: Could it be from a song?
Bill Slater: No, it's not from a song.
Nina Foch: Is it—I'm afraid this has been asked—a poem?
Bill Slater: Yes, it's involved in a poem.
Nina Foch: Is it the innkeeper's daughter? With the long hair? By Noyes, you know?
Bill Slater: No. An interesting girl, the innkeeper's daughter with the long hair. But that's not who it was that we're concerned with.
Florence Rinard: Is this hair?
Bill Slater: No, it's not hair you're after.
Fred Vandeventer: Is this in a poem by a—a rather famous author?
Bill Slater: No.
Fred Vandeventer: In other words, we know it because of the poem and not because of the author?
Bill Slater: I think that's correct, Van.
Florence Rinard: This wouldn't be The Face on the Barroom Floor?
Bill Slater: Florence Rinard!!

Isn't this fun to read? It's even more fun to listen to or play yourself. If you've never played twenty questions, you'd better start right now and find out what you have missed. You can be sure it'll be a long time until you're as expert as the Vandeventers, Herb Polesie or Johnny McPhee.

But, of course, my purpose here is more serious. Twenty questions as I said, is *the* model of productive thinking. How do these experts play the game?

Well, if we analyze those three games, we find three basic rules of twenty questions strategy. They are:

1. Don't waste time with wild stabs.

2. Ask questions that have an even chance of being answered yes or no.

3. Vary your approach.

That wild stabs are bad is rather obvious, of course. Anyone can see that those questions about the Trojan Horse, the California Redwoods and the innkeeper's daughter in *The Highwayman* were sheer waste.

The even-chance principle isn't quite as obvious. Let me explain. Twice, when the subject was vegetable, the radio experts asked first: "Is it wood or a wood product?" Why did they do this? Because they had found by experience that the question "Is it wood?" did not divide the field evenly. If the answer was no, they had to go on and ask "Is it a wood product?" So they developed the combined question "Wood or wood product?" which they knew went just about down the middle of the range of possibilities. Similarly, to narrow down the whole of the United States, they asked first "East or west of the Mississippi?" and then "North or south of the Mason-Dixon line?" To start with the question "East or west of the Hudson River?" would have been poor strategy.

Finally: Vary your approach. It took the panel seven geographical questions to locate those trees in New England; with six more of these questions they could have pinned them down to one particular state. But they were smarter than that. They shifted to the question "What kind of trees?" and went from there directly to the solution.

And now let's see how we can apply the twenty questions technique to thinking in general. In everyday life, of course, we have no M.C. who supplies the yeses and noes; we have to ask *ourselves* each question and answer it as best we can. If we don't know whether the answer is yes or no, we may be able to say "Probably yes" or "Probably no"; if we don't know that either, we may be able to find out. And, of course, we don't have to stick to twenty questions; we may get the solution after only ten, or we may have to ask thirty or forty.

For example, a friend of mine is an engineer who used to work abroad. Recently his company transferred him to their New York City headquarters and he had to find a place to live for himself, his wife and their two boys. This is the kind of problem where you start from scratch, without any kind of lead or clue.

Using the twenty questions method, my friend began to ask himself questions: Do I want a house or an apartment? (A house.) One or two stories? (Two will be all right.) Am I prepared to pay more than $20,000? (No.) More than $15,000? (Rather not.) Shall I commute midtown or downtown? (Downtown.) Am I willing to commute more than twenty miles? (Yes.) More than thirty miles? (Yes.) Will an older house be satisfactory? (No.) Does it have to have a dining room? (Not necessarily.) Do I want a large yard? (Rather.)

After he had asked himself many more questions about locations, communities, neighborhoods, schools, churches, taxes, shopping centers, parks, beaches, and so on, my friend was as close to a solution as he could be while sitting in an armchair and thinking. The rest was easy. He and his family now live happily in a house that's just right for them.

A problem of this sort is not essentially different from a business or industrial problem. For instance, I looked up the section on plant location in an engineering handbook. I found that the engineer has to check, one by one, the following questions: (1) raw materials; (2) fuels and purchased power; (3) labor supply; (4) geographic factors; (5) water resources; (6) transportation facilities and rates; (7) markets; (8) laws and established public practices; (9) special company and industrial policies; and (10) other possible tangible or intangible considerations.

Scientific or industrial research offers some excellent examples of the twenty questions technique. For example, Dr. Flanders Dunbar, in her book *Mind and Body*, tells about a company that operated a large fleet of trucks and became alarmed at a terrific increase in accidents. The management looked into one question after another. They tested everything from the weather to the reaction time of the employees. No success. They tried intensive safety training for the drivers. It didn't help. They tried penalties for those who had accidents and survived. Still the accident rate went on rising.

Finally, the company executives asked themselves whether the accident rate had anything to do with the drivers themselves. So they shifted drivers who had had accidents to work inside the plant. That did it. The problem was solved and the accident rate went down to normal. (The former drivers kept on having accidents in the plant, but that's another story—and a fascinating one too.)

Running through a list of questions or classifications is in fact a characteristic feature of all professional work. Engineers, for instance, use the so-called "search for power" technique and try mentally whether a given problem can be solved electrically, hydraulically, chemically, mechanically, or electronically. Doctors making diagnoses run through lists of diseases with similar symptoms. Lawyers drafting contracts or wills weigh various possibilities of corporate or estate structure. Accountants do the same with different types of accounts, and librarians, of course, with different book classifications.

Not long ago, a book was published that offers a nonprofessional person the sort of helpful check list that every professional carries in his head. It is called *Your Creative Power* and was written by Mr. Alex F. Osborn of the New York advertising firm Batten, Barton, Durstine & Osborn. Mr. Osborn devotes almost one hundred pages to a detailed discussion of his check list of problem-solving questions; you'll learn a lot if you get the book and study those hundred pages carefully. All I can give you here is a brief list of Mr. Osborn's main questions:

To what other uses can this be put?
Is there something similar I could partially copy?
What if this were somewhat changed?
What about making it bigger?
What if this were smaller?
What can I substitute?
How else can this be arranged?
What if this were reversed?
What could I combine this with?

This is an idea-provoking list if there ever was one, but I think it's too much of an advertising man's list to be generally useful. If you follow Mr. Osborn's method of producing ideas, you may wind up with Mr. Osborn's kind of ideas, and they may not always be the right solutions for your problems. He is fond, for instance, of "the Lucky Strike auctioneer, the penguin yodeling 'Kooool' cigarettes, the choo-choo train puffing 'Bromo Seltzer,' the Rinso-white whistle, and the Lifebuoy foghorn," and he is enthusiastic about "a new soap-book, with the story lithographed on the inside cover, and the characters portrayed by illustrations molded on cakes of soap."

Adapting the Osborn list to non-advertising purposes, I have drawn up a little list of my own—the kind of questions that may come in handy in solving such ordinary-life problems as buying a family home. Here it is:

What am I trying to accomplish?
Have I done this sort of thing before? How?

Could I do this some other way?

How did other people tackle this?

What kind of person or persons am I dealing with?

How can this situation be changed to fit me?

How can I adapt myself to this situation?

How about using more? Less? All of it? Only a portion? One only? Two? Several?

How about using something else? Something older? Something newer? Something more expensive? Something cheaper?

How near? How far? In what direction?

How soon? How often? Since when? For how long?

Could I do this in combination? With whom? With what?

How about doing the opposite?

What would happen if I did nothing?

Of course, this list is very general. But you can easily see that it may help in solving everyday problems. In fact, these are the kind of questions everybody asks himself more or less at random; it's useful to have them down in black and white.

However, for an expert twenty questions player a list like this is not enough. It's handy for the opening moves of the game, for the animal-vegetable-mineral or wood-or-wood-product stage. Beyond that, the more unusual the category, the more searching and fruitful the question. To approach The Face on the Barroom Floor, Mr. Vandeventer had to think up a brand-new division of the field: "Little-known poem by famous author or famous poem by little-known author?"

In the same way, the genius problem-solver raises questions that are way beyond the standard repertory. He arrives at a solution by asking himself whether badminton can be played as a noncompetitive game or whether foreign loans can be given in goods rather than money.

Such original classifications are rare, of course. They are hard to think of at the spur of the moment. That's why novel, unusual classifications are always valuable; watch out for them and add them to your mental repertory as you go along.

Collecting unusual classifications is a sort of hobby of mine. Here are some of my more interesting specimens:

E. M. Forster quotes a literary scholar who classified the weather in novels as "decorative, utilitarian, illustrative, planned in pre-established harmony, in emotional contrast, determinative of action, a controlling influence, itself a hero, and non-existent."

Professor Folsom of Vassar College classified love as "sexual, dermal, cardiac-respiratory, and unclassifiable."

Mr. Russell Lynes of *Harper's Magazine* classified people as "high-brows, middle-brows, and low-brows" and as "intellectual snobs, regional snobs, moral snobs, sensual snobs, emotional snobs, taste snobs, occupational snobs, political snobs, and reverse or anti-snob snobs."

Professor W. Lloyd Warner of the University of Chicago classified people socially as "upper-upper-class, lower-upper-class, upper-middle-class, lower-middle-class, upper-lower-class, and lower-lower-class."

Professor Paul F. Lazarsfeld of Columbia University classified people as "opinion leaders and opinion followers."

The German psychiatrist Kretschmer classified people by body types as "pyknic" (round), "asthenic" (thin) and "athletic" (muscular); later Professor William H. Sheldon of Columbia University renamed these types "endomorphs" (fat), "mesomorphs" (strong) and "ectomorphs" (skinny) and called the corresponding temperament types "viscerotonic" (easy-going), "somatotonic" (active) and "cerebrotonic" (nervy).

William James classified people as "tough-minded and tender-minded," C. G. Jung classified them as "introverts and extroverts," and Friedrich Nietzsche classified them as "Dionysian and Apollonian."

And the late Yale geographer Ellsworth Huntington classified people according to what month they were born in, maintaining that most geniuses are conceived in early spring.

The significance of all this for clear thinking and problem-solving isn't always immediately obvious, but it may make quite a difference whether you are dealing with an asthenic, lower-upper-class, middle-brow housewife who was born in April and is a tough-minded opinion leader, or with a viscerotonic, upper-middle-class executive who is an occupational snob and was born an extrovert in November.

Seriously, though, it is true that new classifications will often completely change our attitudes and our thinking.

In the field of nutrition, for instance, the chemical classification of foods has made a vast difference in everybody's eating habits.

In education, the classification of students according to their I.Q. has revolutionized teaching.

In politics, our outlook has changed since the old classification of right *vs.* left has given way to the new one of totalitarian *vs.* democratic.

And history looks different to us since Spengler and Toynbee wrote of the rise and fall of civilizations rather than nations.

All of which may seem pretty far afield from the good old game of twenty questions. But I think the connection is clear. Twenty questions offers a simple strategy for solving everyday problems, but it can also be used to attack and solve the most important problems of our age. As I said, it is the model of modern scientific research technique. Quite possibly, the logic of twenty questions is now the heir to the throne vacated by the logic of the old Greek yes-or-no game.

Future students of twenty questions logic will conceivably start their analysis with a simple mathematical fact: Twenty questions asked by a perfect player cover a range of 1,048,576 possible solutions. In other words, if you know how, you can use twenty questions to pick the one idea in a million.

Now do you believe that twenty questions is a powerful tool of thinking?

CHAPTER 15

The More or Less Scientific Method

In science the important thing is to modify and change one's ideas as science advances.

—Claude Bernard

Perhaps the most famous incident in the history of science occurred in the third century B.C. in Syracuse, Sicily. The mathematician Archimedes was taking a bath. His mind was busy with a scientific problem. King Hiero of Syracuse had ordered a golden crown and suspected the goldsmith of having cheated him by using some silver instead of the gold he'd been supplied with. The king had asked Archimedes to prove it.

Suddenly Archimedes noticed that his body caused some water to spill over. In a flash he realized the solution of the problem: he'd take the crown's weight in pure gold, dip it into water, and see whether the overflow was the same as that of the crown. Whereupon he jumped out of the tub, ran home naked as he was, and shouted to everyone he met: "Eureka! Eureka! . . . I've found it! I've found it!"

Perhaps the *least* famous incident in the history of science occurred in the twentieth century A.D. in the United States. The chemist J. E. Teeple was taking a bath. His mind was busy with a scientific problem. He stepped out of his bath, reached for a towel, dried himself, shaved, took another bath, stepped out of it, reached for a towel and discovered that the towel was wet. Thinking about his scientific problem, he had taken two baths. He had *not* found the solution to his problem.

The first of these incidents has been retold a million times; the second is trivial. Nevertheless, the second is the one that gives the truer picture of the scientific method.

In the first place, the story about Archimedes puts the spotlight on the happy discovery, giving the impression that this sort of thing is typical of a scientist's life. Actually, "Eureka!" moments are few and far between. Einstein once said: "I think and think, for months, for years, ninety-nine times the conclusion is false. The hundredth time I am right." And that's Einstein, the greatest scientific genius of our time. I leave it to you to estimate the percentage of correct solutions in an ordinary scientist's work. Most of their lives are spent like Mr. Teeple's half-hour in the bathroom, thinking and thinking and getting nowhere.

But there's a more important reason why Archimedes crying "Eureka!" isn't a good picture of a scientist. Today no scientist, dressed or undressed, would dream of telling people "I've found it!" as soon as he has hit upon a bright idea. Even less would he do the modern equivalent—announce his discovery immediately to the press. Just the contrary. He would take care not to breathe a word about it to anyone, but quietly go to his laboratory and run some tests—and more tests—and more tests.

A scientist today doesn't consider a bright idea as a revelation of the truth; he considers it as something to be disproved. Not just proved, mind you; it's his obligation as a scientist to think of every conceivable means and ways to *dis*prove it. This habit is so ingrained in him that he doesn't even realize it any more; he automatically thinks of a theory as something to find flaws in. So he does experiments and hunts for every error he can possibly think of; and when he is through with his own experiments, he publishes his findings not in a newspaper but in a scientific journal, inviting other scientists to do some other experiments and prove him wrong.

And when the hunt for errors has subsided and a theory gets established and accepted—do scientists think they've got hold of a new truth? No. To them, all scientific findings are only *tentative* truths, "good until further notice," to be immediately discarded when someone comes along with another theory that explains a few more facts. Absolute truth doesn't even interest them; they get along very happily, thank you, with a set of working hypotheses that are good only at certain times and for certain purposes. The most famous example of this today is the theory of light. There is a wave theory that fits certain investigations, and a particle theory that fits certain others. Years ago physicists stopped trying to find out which is true and which is false. The Danish Nobel prize winner, Niels Bohr, has called this the principle of complementarity, saying that after all "waves" and "particles" are only handy metaphors in dealing with certain facts; so why not use whichever is more practical at the moment? Never mind what light is "really"; let's get on with the job of finding out what it *does*. Or, as one physicist said, "Let's use the particle theory on Mondays, Wednesdays, and Fridays, and the wave theory on Tuesdays, Thursdays, and Saturdays."

For the layman, the most important thing about science is this: that it isn't a search for truth but a search for error. The scientist lives in a world where truth is unattainable, but where it's always possible to find errors in the long-settled or the obvious. You want to know whether some theory is really scientific? Try this simple test: If the thing is shot through with *perhapses* and *maybe's* and hemming and hawing, it's probably science; if it's supposed to be *the* final answer, it is not.

So-called "scientific" books that are supposed to contain final answers are never scientific. Science is forever self-correcting and changing; what is put forth as gospel truth cannot be science.

But what does *science* mean? If someone asked you for a definition, you'd probably be on the spot. If pressed, you might come up with something like the definition in Webster's: "A branch of study . . . concerned with the observation and classification of facts, esp. with the establishment . . . of verifiable general laws . . ."

That's a pretty good description of what the word means to the average person. Does it mean the same thing to scientists? It does not. Recently President Conant of Harvard, a chemist, published *his* definition of science: "An interconnected series of concepts and conceptual schemes that have developed as a result of experimentation and observation and are fruitful of further experimentation and observation." As you see, the two definitions are almost exact opposites. *You* think science deals with facts; a scientist thinks it deals with concepts. *You* think science tries to establish laws; a scientist thinks it aims at more and more experiments.

And what is the scientific method? Your answer is apt to be: "The classification of facts." President Conant's answer is again different. Look up *Scientific method* in the index of his book, and you'll find this: "Scientific method. *See* Alleged scientific method." In other words, President Conant thinks there *isn't any* scientific method.

That surely is extreme. Even if there is no clearly definable scientific method, there's a way in which scientists work, and it's certainly worth knowing about. Let's look at a careful description by Dr. W. I. B. Beveridge, a British biologist:

The following is a common sequence in an investigation of a medical or biological problem:

(*a*) The relevant literature is critically reviewed.

(*b*) A thorough collection of field data or equivalent observational enquiry is conducted, and is supplemented if necessary by laboratory examination of specimens.

(*c*) The information obtained is marshalled and correlated and the problem is defined and broken down into specific questions.

(*d*) Intelligent guesses are made to answer the questions, as many hypotheses as possible being considered.

(*e*) Experiments are devised to test first the likeliest hypotheses bearing on the most crucial questions.

The key word here is *guesses* in (*d*). In the popular view the emphasis is on (*b*), the collection of data. But not among scientists. They like to distinguish between "accumulators" and "guessers," and they're pretty much agreed that it's the guessers that are important. In more fancy terms, you could say that the modern emphasis is on deduction rather than induction, or that the Aristotelian method is now more esteemed than the Baconian. What it comes down to is simply this: Our top scientists say we need more ideas rather than more facts; they want more Einsteins who just sit and think rather than Edisons who have a genius for tinkering in the laboratory. After all, Edison, as one of them has said, "was not a scientist and was not even interested in science."

Meanwhile, our research relies far more on accumulating than on guessing. General Electric, with its training courses in "Creative Engineering," is the exception; the American Cancer Society, which is openly resigned to "whittling away at this mass of mystery," is typical of the general rule.

Which is why Dr. Sinnott, director of the Sheffield School of Science at Yale, said recently:

It must be ruefully admitted that we have not produced our share of great new germinative ideas in recent years. In atomic research, for example, most of the fundamental theoretical progress was made either by European scientists or men who had received their training abroad. We are strong in application, in development and engineering, but much less so in the fundamental contributions of the theory on which all these are based. . . . We are in danger of being overwhelmed by a mass of undigested results.

And what is the method used by those hard-to-find "guessers"? If we try to analyze it, we come right back to Duncker's description of problem-solving, to his "solutions from below" and "solutions from above." Scientific problems are solved either by finding a seemingly irrelevant key factor or by applying a seemingly unsuitable thought pattern. Which means that scientific discoveries are made in one of two ways: by accident or by hunch.

Take any history of science, and you'll find that it is a history of accidents and hunches. Both types of discoveries are equally fascinating.

If you're interested in accidents, for instance, scientific history looks like this:

In 1786, Luigi Galvani noticed the accidental twitching of a frog's leg and discovered the principle of the electric battery.

In 1822, the Danish physicist Oersted, at the end of a lecture, happened to put a wire conducting an electric current near a magnet, which led to Faraday's invention of the electric dynamo.

In 1858, a seventeen-year-old boy named William Henry Perkin, trying to make artificial quinine, cooked up a black-looking mass, which led to his discovery of aniline dye.

In 1889, Professors von Mering and Minkowski operated on a dog. A laboratory assistant noticed that the dog's urine attracted swarms of flies. He called this to the attention of Minkowski, who found that the urine contained sugar. This was the first step in the control of diabetes.

In 1895, Roentgen noticed that cathode rays penetrated black paper and discovered X-rays.

In 1929, Sir Alexander Fleming noticed that a culture of bacteria had been accidentally contaminated by a mold. He said to himself: "My, that's a funny thing." He had discovered penicillin.

Of course, all these accidents would have been meaningless if they hadn't happened to Galvani, Perkin, Roentgen, and so on. As Pasteur has said, "Chance favors the prepared mind." What is necessary is an accidental event plus an observer with *serendipity*—"the gift of finding valuable or agreeable things not sought for." (Horace Walpole coined that beautiful word.)

On the other hand, if you're interested in hunches, scientific history looks like this, for example:

Harvey describes his discovery of the circulation of the blood:

I frequently and seriously bethought me, and long revolved in my mind, what might be the quantity of blood which was transmitted, in how short a time its passage might be effected and the like. . . . I began to think whether there might not be a motion, as it were, in a circle.

James Watt invents the steam engine:

On a fine Sabbath afternoon I took a walk. . . . I had entered the green and had passed the old washing house. I was thinking of the engine at the time. I had gone as far as the herd's house when the idea came into my mind that as steam was an elastic body it would rush into a vacuum, and if a connection were made between the cylinder and an exhausting vessel it would rush into it and might then be condensed without cooling the cylinder. . . . I had not walked further than the golf house when the whole thing was arranged in my mind.

Darwin writes about his theory of evolution:

I can remember the very spot in the road, whilst in my carriage, when to my joy the solution occurred to me.

Kekulé tells how he discovered the benzene ring on top of a London bus:

I sank into a reverie. The atoms flitted about before my eyes. . . . I saw how two small ones often joined into a little pair; how a larger took hold of two smaller, and a still larger clasped three or even four of the small ones, and how all spun around in a whirling round-dance. . . . The cry of the conductor, "Clapham Road," woke me up.

Walter B. Cannon discovers the significance of bodily changes in fear and rage:

These changes—the more rapid pulse, the deeper breathing, the increase of sugar in the blood, the secretion from the adrenal glands—were very diverse and seemed unrelated. Then, one wakeful night, after a considerable collection of these changes had been disclosed, the idea flashed through my mind that they could be nicely integrated if conceived as bodily preparations for supreme effort in flight or in fighting.

Does all this mean that some scientists are good at hunches and some others blessed with serendipity? Not at all. The accidental clue needs a receptive mind; the hunch has to grow from a study of facts. The good guesser works both ways, depending on what he has to go on. Here's one more example that shows a combination of both methods. It is typical of modern scientific research in many ways.

During World War II, a team of psychologists studied the propaganda effect of orientation films. Among other things, they tried to find out whether films changed the opinions and attitudes of soldiers who saw them, and whether and how these changes lasted. They had a hunch that the effect of the films would gradually wear off and that after some time, soldiers would forget the factual details and revert to their original opinion.

This idea may seem rather obvious to you. It seemed obvious to the psychologists too—but, being scientists, they decided to test it anyway. So they gave the soldiers a test after one week and another test after nine weeks.

As expected, the soldiers had forgotten most of the facts in the film during those eight weeks. But, "clearly contrary to the initial expectation," the general propaganda effect of the film—the opinion change—had considerably *increased* between the first and the second test. There was not the slightest doubt about it: the soldiers had forgotten the details of the film, but its message had sunk in deeper.

The research team cheerfully accepted this unexpected fact and immediately proceeded to account for it by a hypothesis. They found that it could be explained through a theory by the British psychologist, Bartlett, published in 1932. Bartlett had written that "after learning, that which is recalled tends to be modified with lapse of time in the direction of omission of all but general content and introduction of new material in line with the individual's attitudes." In other words, as time passes, we're apt to forget details but *reinforce* what we remember of the general idea.

Well, what have we here? Doubtless the research team made a valuable discovery. Yet the whole story is as unlike that of Archimedes in his bath as can be. For one thing, there is no single scientist, but a team of thirteen men and two women. Second, the discovery is exactly the opposite from what the scientists expected to find. Third, it is immediately connected up with an idea thought up by another scientist in another country, twenty years before.

And finally, there is no "Eureka!", no shouting from the housetops, no happy announcement to the world. Instead, after reporting their discovery and stating their hypothesis, the researchers add casually: "These highly speculative suggestions indicate some very interesting areas for future research."

CHAPTER 16

The Harnessing of Chance

It is better to be satisfied with probabilities than to demand impossibilities and starve.

—F. C. S. Schiller

The wildly improbable happens every day.

Not long ago there was a picture in *Life* that showed a group of deer including three albinos. Photographer Staber Reese took it in northern Wisconsin, where there are 850,000 white-tailed deer, twenty of which are albinos. Reese figured that the mathematical odds against a picture with three albino deer in it were 79 billion to one.

Or consider the odd coincidences that happen in everyone's life. For example, on page 39 of this book I listed some of the Chukchee names for reindeer. I had found these names referred to (but not given) in a book by Franz Boas, and went to the New York Public Library to copy them from Boas' source—the tattered, fifty-year-old seventh volume of the report on the Jesup North Pacific Expedition by Waldemar Bogoras. When I came home that evening, I found the latest copy of *The New Yorker*. The first thing I read in it was a "footloose correspondent" report on Lapland, listing the various names for reindeer used by the Lapps.

Or here is something a little more exotic. In 1923 the poet and literary scholar Leonard Bacon went to the University of California library and took out a twenty-year-old book published in Vienna. On the train to Monterey, he opened the book and began to read the introduction. When he got to the acknowledgments, he came upon the arresting name Lord Talbot de Malahide. (This was long before the Boswell papers were found at Malahide Castle.) At this point Mr. Bacon got bored with his book and turned to the San Francisco *Chronicle*. There he found a social note that Lord and Lady Talbot de Malahide were staying at the St. Francis Hotel.

Too trivial for you? Then consider the following case. In 1908 the Rev. James Smith, pastor of a small Negro congregation at Reid's Ferry, Virginia, mysteriously disappeared. Soon afterward the corpse of a large Negro was found in the Nansemond River near the church. There was evidence of a blow on the head with a blunt instrument. The body was unrecognizable, but its clothes were identified as similar to those worn by Smith. Also, a woman friend of Smith who had not seen the body told the authorities that if it was Smith, they'd find a ring with a purple setting on the little finger of the left hand. They did.

The most likely suspect of the murder was Smith's rival and successor, the Rev. Ernest Lyons. He was tried, convicted of second-degree murder, and sentenced to eighteen years in prison.

Three years later Smith was found alive in North Carolina, where he had absconded with church funds. He wore a ring with a purple setting on the little finger of his left hand. The fateful ring on the corpse in the river had been sheer coincidence. Lyons had served three years in prison for "murdering" a man who was still alive.

There is no complete defense against the sea of improbabilities that surrounds us. But there are weapons. Armed with probability theory and statistics, it is possible to face calmly this world of coincidences and seemingly miraculous events.

Above all, the statistical approach is an antidote against the shudder and the helplessness we feel in the face of the extraordinary. Mr. Reese figured that the chances against his getting that deer picture were 79 billion to one. He may have been wrong, of course; but even if he was right, the oddest of chances is a more comfortable thing to contemplate than something that cannot possibly happen but does. At the Monte Carlo roulette table, red once came up thirty-two times in a row. This must have been an uncanny thing to watch for those who were there, but they too had the comfort of knowing that it wasn't a miracle. It was just something that happens once in four billion times.

The other way round, the statistical approach is also helpful because it teaches you that you can't always expect the average. Don't believe it if people tell you that statisticians reduce everything to averages. It just isn't so: they know better than anyone else that an average is just one point on a curve.

In short, the statistical view gives you a pretty realistic picture of what the world is like. We are all apt to assume that the good, the bad and the medium are fairly evenly distributed; but the statisticians can prove that this is wrong. Their bell-shaped, so-called "normal" curve shows that ordinarily there are more medium cases than either good or bad ones, and there are always some that are *very* good or *very* bad. Suppose you are interested in girls and classify them as "good-looking," "plain" and "so-so." Do you expect to find about one-third of each? A statistician will tell you that you mustn't overlook the exceptional cases at either end of the scale and that you must be prepared to see more of the average. His "normal" distribution will look like this:

Beautiful	7 per cent
Good-looking	24 per cent
So-so	38 per cent
Plain	24 per cent
Ugly	7 per cent

Look around you, and you'll find that statisticians know a thing or two.

Most important, statistics teaches you not to rely on a single instance, or even a few. You need lots of cases to establish a fact—not as true, mind you, but as highly probable. One case is nothing; ten cases are nothing. A thousand cases? Maybe they show a trend.

But then, of course, it's not always possible to assemble a thousand cases, and even if you do, you're apt to run into errors and mistakes. The larger the figures, the larger the sources of error. In July, 1950, Dr. Roy V. Peel, national director of the Census Bureau, revealed that even with the best scientific methods census figures "should be within about one percent of the truth." In September, 1949, the U.S. Bureau of Labor Statistics discovered it had underrated the number of unemployed by one million.

So, since complete surveys aren't practical and far from foolproof, statisticians are usually content to take samples. In theory, a small random sample tells almost as much as a full survey. But there is a joker in this statement: it's the word *random*.

If you draw slips with names from a drum, it's supposedly random. But even in that case statisticians will tell you that certain elements may influence your choice. What you think is random—like closing your eyes and dropping a pencil on a page—isn't random to a statistician at all. They use printed tables of random numbers, and even with those they're always afraid of some bias creeping in somewhere.

For instance, statisticians have discovered that three-fourths of the population are apt to call "heads" rather than "tails" in coin tossing. Why, nobody knows. They have found that if you arrange five test questions so that the correct answers are "yes," "no," "yes," "no," "yes," people will unconsciously shy away from that pattern. Looks too symmetrical to be right. They have found that if you pick a sample of people whose name begins with a certain letter, the sample will be biased. Names are connected with nationality, and therefore with income and social status.

In social surveys and public opinion polls, random sampling seems to be particularly impossible. True, there is a new system—"area sampling"—that excludes the interviewer's bias and forces him to question certain people whether he wants to or not; but even that method is far from foolproof. The older system—"quota sampling"—leaves it to the interviewer to make up his quota of interviewees. This is the method of the Gallup poll and most other public opinion polls. It *never* produces a random sample. When you stop to think about it, that's quite obvious, since interviewers are just like other people and dislike dirt, noise, smells, sickness, stair-climbing, unfriendliness, language difficulties and all the other embarrassments and troubles that make up a truly random sample. No wonder there are about 15 per cent more well-educated, native-born, one-family-house dwellers in most quota samples than there are in the American population.

I don't mean to say that public opinion polls are useless. On the contrary, they are miraculously successful, considering what they're up against. They are a wonderful tool of social science—and getting better and better as the problems of random sampling are gradually being explored and solved.

All of this, however, is comparatively simple. Statistics gets really complicated when we get into the business of two-way statistics—in other words, correlations. This is where we get into the statistical solution of problems.

To understand what correlation is all about, let's go back for a moment to that nineteenth-century genius, John Stuart Mill—the man whose I.Q. was estimated the highest of all time; the man who learned ancient Greek at the age of three. Having read Aristotle's logic in the original when he was twelve, Mill thought that something ought to be

done about it. After some twenty-five years, he did: in 1843 he published his own *Logic* as a substitute.

Aristotle, as we have seen, started with the analysis of the yes-or-no
game; Mill, more sensibly, started with an analysis of the methods used
in scientific research. So, instead of the old rules of the syllogism, he
came up with four methods of experimental inquiry. These, he proudly
announced, were the only possible ones—"at least, I know not, nor am
I able to imagine, any others. . . . They compose the available resources
of the human mind for ascertaining the laws of the succession of
phenomena."

Now what are Mill's "methods"? Basically, there are two: the "method
of agreement" and the "method of difference"—which may be combined
into the "joint method of agreement *and* difference." There are also
two more specialized methods: the "method of residues" and the
"method of concomitant variations." Mill explains all these with great
complexity and Early Victorian detail, but fortunately we don't have
to bother with all that. By the time John Dewey got around to writing
his book on *How We Think* in 1910, Mill's rules were just good enough
for a brief footnote, stating casually that only the "joint method of agreement and difference" was of any use. Well, the "joint method of agreement and difference" consists simply in varying one factor while
keeping all others constant. Long ago it was phrased unsurpassably by
Professor C. F. Chandler of Columbia University: "Vary one thing at
a time, and make a note of all you do."

The effect of this—of varying one thing at a time—can be measured
by the statistical technique of correlation. You take a large number of
cases, measure the variable you are interested in, measure another
variable for comparison, and work out the relationship between the two.
Basically, it's nothing but a refinement of the kind of thing you do
naturally to find the cause of any effect. If you sit under a lamp and
the light goes out, you fetch another bulb and screw it in: you vary
one factor, keeping everything else constant. If the new bulb works,
you're satisfied you've found the cause of the light going out. If it
doesn't, you vary other factors, one at a time: you try another plug, you
change a fuse, and so on. Each step is a scientific experiment in
miniature.

So far, so good. But often you do the same thing *without* experiment-
ing. You see that a change in one factor is accompanied by a certain
effect, and you think you've discovered the cause. This is Mill's method

of "concomitant variations." It may work—sometimes; or it may not. Since you didn't set up the experiment, you can't control anything; and the effect may have been produced by a million reasons you don't know of.

For example, there is the classic case of the village of Polykastron in Greece. Early in 1950 the United Nations International Children's Emergency Fund distributed powdered milk to expectant mothers there. Shortly afterward, the first two women who used it gave birth to twins on the same day—the first twins born in the village in ten years. The women of Polykastron drew the obvious conclusion; they decided they'd rather *not* use UN powdered milk.

Why, these were poor Greek peasant women, you say: educated people are not apt to make such mistakes. But they do. Conspicuous correlations fool everybody, including scientists. For instance, in 1927 Dr. Manfred Sakel discovered that schizophrenia can be treated by administering overdoses of insulin. Overdoses of insulin often produce a convulsive shock. So hundreds of psychiatrists, just like the Greek women, drew the obvious conclusion and began to treat schizophrenia and other mental diseases by simply giving their patients electric shocks and leaving out the insulin. At a 1950 psychiatric convention, Dr. Sakel sadly explained that electric shocks are actually harmful and that the insulin cure is really based on restoring a patient's balance of hormones. For over twenty years, he said, the standard procedure had been based on a misconception.

This is the sort of thing to keep in mind before putting too much faith in correlations. Statisticians have even more impressive examples. One of them discovered a correlation of .90 between the number of storks' nests in Stockholm and the number of babies born there over a period of years. Another (this was a favorite example of the late Professor Morris Cohen) found, over a certain period, a correlation of .87 between the membership of the International Machinists' Union and the death rate of the state of Hyderabad.

You want to know the meaning of these figures? They look like percentages but they are not: they are correlation coefficients. Let's spend a minute or two on getting the hang of the basic principle.

Correlation coefficients come in assorted sizes between plus one and minus one. Plus one means perfect correlation: if *x* happens, *y* always happens too. Minus one means perfect negative correlation: if *x* happens, *y* never happens. Zero means no correlation whatever: if *x* happens, *y* may or may not happen, you can't tell.

For example, let's take some fictitious correlation coefficients between *age* and *value*:

+.90: Value regularly increases with age (e.g. wine)

+.45: Value often increases with age (e.g. paintings)

.00: Value has nothing to do with age (e.g. diamonds)

—.45: Value often decreases with age (e.g. houses)

—.90: Value regularly decreases with age (e.g. news)

I didn't give examples of plus one or minus one, because perfect correlations virtually don't exist. Statisticians consider a correlation of .90 (like that between Stockholm storks' nests and babies) as practically perfect.

And now that I have given you proper warning against putting blind faith in correlations, let me show you what they are good for.

Take, for instance, a recent analysis of certain intelligence tests for boys who wanted to qualify for the Army or Navy college training program during World War II. Researchers figured the averages of the scores for each of the forty-eight states and correlated those averages with other statistics. Here are some of their findings:

+.83: Intelligence test scores increased with number of telephones per thousand.

+.69: Intelligence test scores increased with number of foreign-born per thousand.

+.67: Intelligence test scores increased with number of residents per 100,000 in *Who's Who.*

—.01: Intelligence test scores had nothing to do with number of persons killed in auto accidents per 100,000.

—.53: Intelligence test scores decreased with percentage of population without library service.

—.53: Intelligence test scores decreased with number of lynchings (1882-1944) per 100,000.

—.66: Intelligence test scores decreased with number of rural homes without privies per 1,000.

"Without much facetiousness," the researchers summed up, "we interpret these results to mean that the probabilities of reaching a high educational achievement are much greater if one comes from a high income state which is highly urban, which is not in the South, and which has such advantages as library service available to most of its population, has a high proportion of foreign-born citizens, a large number of residents in *Who's Who,* and many telephones."

Or take another recent study by Dr. Sheldon Glueck of Harvard University and his wife, Dr. Eleanor Glueck. They tried to find the causes of juvenile delinquency. More scientifically speaking, they tried to isolate certain factors that distinguish delinquent boys from those who are not.

Dr. and Mrs. Glueck devoted ten years to their study. Being scientists, they began their study by making certain guesses. Being scientists, they then proceeded to test these guesses. They assembled mountains of data on five hundred delinquent and five hundred nondelinquent boys. When they had collected all the statistics on the factors they were interested in, they looked for differences in the degree of correlation.

They found, among other things, that the parents of delinquent boys were often more erratic than those of other boys; that between-children are more likely to become delinquent than either first or last children; that delinquent boys were usually more muscular than others and scored higher in certain parts of intelligence tests. On the whole, they found that delinquency is connected with a boy's home life, with his temperament and character, and with his ability to get along with people. In fact, Dr. and Mrs. Glueck drew up a "prediction table" by which six-year-olds can be spotted as future delinquents if a long list of factors is known. But, of course, they didn't say that this prediction was infallible or that they had found once and for all the causes of juvenile delinquency. They just reported what they gingerly called a "tentative causal formula or law."

Now this is exactly the kind of thing people are apt to explain by "fate" or "bad blood" or "slum conditions" or whatever other pet explanation they are fond of. The Glueck study is a beautiful example of the scientific approach. The Gluecks didn't look for a single cause; in fact, they didn't look for "a cause" at all. They looked for certain factors that were to a certain degree connected with delinquency. And they concluded, *not* that juvenile delinquency was due to this or that, but that if a combination of certain factors was present to a certain degree, the result would probably be a tendency to delinquency.

Of course I don't mean to say that in everyday life you shouldn't decide anything before you have made a ten-year statistical study. But you can use the scientific approach as a model. Instead of the black-

and-white, single-track, everyone-knows-that-this-is-due-to-that approach, get used to the idea that this is a world of multiple causes, imperfect correlations, and sheer, unpredictable chance.

It is true that the scientists, with their statistics and their probabilities, have made a stab at the harnessing of chance. But they know very well that certainty is unattainable. A high degree of probability is the best we can ever get.

CHAPTER 17

How Not to Rack Your Brain

"The horror of that moment," the King went on, "I shall never, *never* forget!"

"You will, though," the Queen said, "if you don't make a memorandum of it."

—Lewis Carroll, *Through the Looking Glass*

It's time to take a long breath.

Have we gotten any closer to clear thinking after our excursions into logic, law, psychology, science and statistics? Have we arrived at any rules?

Well, if you've learned anything from this book so far, you'll know that there can't *be* any rules. Or rather, that the first rule of clear thinking is not to go by rules.

However, let's stop for a moment and at least draw up a list of reminders from the preceding chapters. Here it is:

1. Try to remember that everybody, including yourself, has only his own experience to think with.

2. Try to detach your ideas from your words.

3. Translate the abstract and general into the concrete and specific.

4. Don't apply general rules blindly to specific problems.

5. To solve a puzzling problem, look for a seemingly irrelevant key factor in the situation and for a seemingly unsuitable pattern in your mind.

6. Narrow the field of solutions by asking "twenty questions."

7. Remember that bright ideas are often wrong and must be tested.

8. Don't underrate the influence of chance.

If you are the kind of person who likes advice highly concentrated and neatly packaged, this is about the best I can do for you.

Except for one thing. The art of thinking, like every other art, has also an element of sheer routine about it—the basic mechanics of the thing—when to do precisely what in what way. The art of writing, for instance, includes, at a lower level, penmanship or typing; the art of painting, a knowledge of brushes and paints. In the same way, the art of thinking includes a certain amount of mechanics: when to think; where to find ideas; how to use thinking tools. So, while it is impossible to draw up a list of thinking rules, it is quite possible to give you some definite, practical thinking *tips*.

To begin with, there are what is known as "stages of thought." There is a typical, known sequence to the production of ideas—a sequence that is the same whether the product is a symphony, a mathematical theorem, a treaty or an advertisement. The literature on this fascinating subject reads like nothing else on earth; it's a branch of psychology, but it was written by chemists, novelists, mathematicians, biologists, poets and a very few psychologists. It is studded with case histories of artistic and intellectual creation, from Descartes and Mozart to Einstein and Thomas Wolfe. It has two great classics: Professor John Livingston Lowes' monumental study of how Coleridge created his poem *Kubla Khan*, and Henri Poincaré's famous lecture on how he arrived at the theory of Fuchsian functions.

Among other things, this literature contains at least a dozen descriptions of "stages of thought," all somewhat similar. Here are four of them:

First, the four stages listed in *The Art of Thought* by Graham Wallas, a political scientist:

1. Preparation—the stage during which the problem is investigated.
2. Incubation—the stage during which you are not consciously thinking about the problem.
3. Illumination—the appearance of the "happy idea."
4. Verification.

Next, the five stages of Mr. James Webb Young, an advertising man who wrote a little book, *A Technique for Producing Ideas*:

1. The gathering of raw materials—both the materials of your immediate problem and the materials which come from a constant enrich-ment of your store of general knowledge.
2. The working over of these materials in your mind.

3. The incubating stage—where you let something beside the conscious mind do the work of synthesis.

4. The actual birth of the Idea—the "Eureka! I have it!" stage.

5. The final shaping and developing of the idea to practical usefulness.

Third, the four stages of Mr. J. F. Young, of the General Electric Company, who is interested in "Developing Creative Engineers":

1. Definition of the problem.

2. Manipulation of elements bearing on solution.

3. Period resulting in the intuitive idea.

4. The idea is shaped to practical usefulness.

Fourth, the stages listed by a psychologist, Dr. Eliot Dole Hutchinson:

1. Preparation or orientation.

2. Frustration, renunciation or recession, in which for a time the problem is given up.

3. The period or moment of insight.

4. Verification, elaboration or evaluation.

On the whole, however, psychologists aren't too fond of this sort of approach. Take for instance the 1950 president of the American Psychological Association, Dr. J. P. Guilford of the University of Southern California. In his presidential address he said, with an air of marked distaste:

In the writings of those who have attempted to give a generalized picture of creative behavior, there is considerable agreement that the complete creative act involves four important steps. . . . The creator begins with a period of preparation, devoted to an inspection of his problem and a collection of information or material. There follows a period of incubation during which there seems to be little progress in the direction of fulfillment. But, we are told, there *is* activity, only it is mostly unconscious. There eventually comes the big moment of inspiration, with a final, or semi-final solution, often accompanied by strong emotions. There usually follows a period of evaluation or verification, in which the creator tests the solution or examines the product for its fitness or value. Little or much touching up may be done to the product.

Dr. Guilford adds:

Such an analysis is very superficial from the psychological point of view. It is more dramatic than it is suggestive of testable hypotheses. It tells us almost nothing about the mental operations that actually occur. The concepts do not lead directly to test ideas . . .

Well, that puts Messrs. Lowes, Poincaré, Wallas, J. W. Young, J. F. Young, Hutchinson et al. in their places, but it also gives us an excellent summary of the "considerable agreement" on the stages of thought. Dr. Guilford may not like it, but the body of evidence for the four stages of thought is there, for all to see.

And now that we have a good composite picture of the thinking process, let's see how we can practically improve the mechanics of each stage.

Let's start with Mr. J. F. Young's first step, the definition of the problem. For this I can give you four practical tips:

1. *Write the problem down.* The most important tools for a problem-solver are pencil and paper. If you want evidence for this obvious proposition, take my friends and students who were exposed to the two little problems on page 105. Among the solutions done on paper, 80 per cent were right; among those done in the head, 88 per cent were wrong.

2. *Translate the problem into simple language.* All translation helps; translation into concrete, plain language helps most. J. B. S. Haldane, the famous biologist, claimed that he made many of his discoveries while writing popular-science articles for factory workers.

3. *If the problem can be stated mathematically, state it mathematically.* Mathematics is a treasure house of problem-solving formulas. If you can use it, by all means do so. If you don't know enough mathematics, pass the problem on to someone who does.

4. *If the problem can be stated graphically, state it graphically.* A graph often helps you understand something that looks unintelligible in words or figures. Louis Bean, the only man who has been consistently right in predicting election results, says he performs this magic trick with charts and graphs. Again, if you are not up on this technique, pass the problem on to someone who is.

Next, let's proceed to the preparation stage. The first practical tip here is simple but basic: *Don't rely on your memory.*

In Chapter 3 I tried to show you that everyone's memory is unreliable. But as if this wasn't enough trouble, we usually remember the trivial and forget the essential.

Of course you know what silly little things we remember. W. W. Sawyer, an English mathematician, sums it up nicely:

There are hundreds of things—odd remarks, pointless little stories, tricks with matches, stray pieces of information—which seem to have no use in life, but which stay in your memory for years. At school we read a history book. . . . No one remembers the history. . . . But there were certain footnotes in it; one about a curate who grew crops in the churchyard and said it would be turnips next year; a lady who blacked out a picture and said "She is blacker within"; a verse about someone longing to be at 'em and waiting for the Earl of Chatham—everyone knew these years after they left school.

These are the things we remember. And what are the things we forget? At school you learned how to find a square root. Can you do it now? I can't. I bet you can't either.

For your comfort, let me quote the great mathematician Henri Poincaré: "I am absolutely incapable of adding without mistakes." And the famous writer Somerset Maugham: "I often think how much easier life would have been for me and how much time I should have saved if I had known the alphabet. I can never tell where I and J stand without saying G, H to myself first. I don't know whether P comes before R or after, and where T comes in has to this day remained something that I have never been able to get into my head."

Alekhine, the late world chess champion, once played fifteen blind games simultaneously. After some time he asked an umpire for a cigarette. "How absent-minded of me!" he said. "I left my cigarette case at home again!"

So this is the main instrument we have for thinking. Here's a fair example of how it works in an actual case. Miss May Lamberton Becker, the well-known conductor of "The Reader's Guide" in the New York *Herald-Tribune*, once got the following inquiry from a reader:

Many years ago I read a novel which I should like to read again. I do not remember the title or the author. . . . It was an English novel and the chief character was a man. I believe he had a title, but I'm not sure about that. He was perfectly formed from the waist up but his legs were abnormally short.

Miss Becker described the process by which she arrived at the answer:

There's no use making a strong effort at recall. It is like sitting beside a small, dark pool, keeping your eye fixed on it and expecting something to come up. What had come up immediately, like a bubble to the surface, was a sense of repulsion, something remembered as monstrous. Then . . . I knew I'd read it years ago, early in the century. Then . . . it was written by somebody using a pseudonym—a short one—foreign-sounding . . . a man's but the writer was a woman. Then . . . the word *Sir* began to emerge from the submerged title; the sense of getting warmer was so strong I went to Keller's *Reader's Digest of Books* and found in no time that it was *The History of Sir Richard Calmady* by Lucas Malet, the daughter of Charles Kingsley, Mrs. Harrison. The whole jerky process went so rapidly that the book was recovered in less than eight minutes.

The moral is clear: *Don't rely on your memory but use written or printed sources.* Half the secret of good thinking is the intelligent use of sources.

Luckily for you, the use of source materials is easier today than ever before. In the last fifty years there has been a sort of revolution; it is a thousand times easier for you today to use source materials than it was for Aristotle, Bacon, Descartes, Newton, Goethe or any other great thinker of the past.

This sounds exaggerated but it is true. Up to some fifty years ago, bibliography—the hunting of sources—was something every thinker had to do for himself. If he was lucky, he found what he needed; if not, he missed it. Gregor Mendel's experiments in heredity were published in 1866; in 1900 they had to be rediscovered by Correns, de Vries and Tschermak-Seysenegg.

Today such a thing couldn't happen. Every branch of science is covered bibliographically, and every scientist automatically follows the bibliography of his field. And this is not all. You, the layman, can now prepare your thoughts exactly like a scientist. The results of scientific thinking are regularly transmitted to you. Scientists rarely bother to tell laymen about their findings; but scores of popularizers now study scientific bibliographies and pass on to the layman everything he ought to know.

There's no excuse any more for by-passing published information; the sum of the world's recorded knowledge is as near as the nearest library. If you can't get to a library, you can write or phone; if the material you want isn't there, you can get it through interlibrary loan.

Of course, reading books, magazines and newspapers is only half the job. The other half is using all this material in place of that wretched memory of yours. This means note-taking and filing. How you do it is up to you; pick your own system. But note-taking and filing there has to be; practically all the world's ideas have come out of notes and files.

The book you are reading now came out of a file drawer with twenty-one folders—one for each chapter. Something like this file drawer is behind almost every book in existence—including even humor books. (The late Will Cuppy amassed and filed hundreds of three-by-five index cards before writing each of his charming essays on topics like the minnow or the dodo.)

But don't get the impression that the first stage of thinking is always a solitary game of shuffling index cards. There's a more sociable way of drawing on other people's thoughts: the discussion method.

Discussion method, of course, is only a fancy name for conversation. To shape your thoughts, exchange ideas with others. Have a group of people sit around and talk, and you'll find that together they'll have more ideas than each of them separately. This is a clear case of the whole being more than its parts. Conversation is the greatest idea generator known to man.

It is impossible to overrate the idea-producing power of conversation. Some of the best education is "Mark Hopkins on one end of the log and James Garfield on the other"; some of the shrewdest business deals are those arranged over the luncheon table; some of the greatest scientific discoveries have come out of informal chats at annual meetings.

Are there any rules for idea-producing conversation? Well, a few are obvious: keep the talk on the subject; let everyone contribute something; take notes of what has been said. A few are not so obvious: don't forget to sum up once in a while; don't be afraid of pauses. The most important rule of all is this: when you're not talking, listen. Don't sit there, unhearing, rehearsing what you're going to say next.

How many people should there be in the group? The minimum, of course, is two; but what is the maximum? There is no answer, except that everyone should have a chance to say something. Put a dozen people in a room, and you'll find that four or five hardly open their mouths.

What's the best composition of the group? Again, there's no answer. But try to get as many viewpoints as possible. Get the young and the old together, executives and wage earners, farmers and professors, men and women.

Now suppose you have done your library work, assembled your notes, talked with others. Are you through with the preparation stage? Not quite. There are a few more things you can do to help your ideas to the surface.

First, remember the twenty questions technique. Practically, this means: Use a check list. Just a few days ago I made out my income tax return. When I went over the check list of deductions, I came upon

Thefts and Losses and remembered that last summer my camera had been stolen. Result: About $12 saved. See?

Don't stick to a set list of classifications, though. Add new ones. Shuffle your index cards around; redistribute the material in your folders. If you find a promising new category, add it to the list; it'll come in handy some time. Recently, *The New Yorker* ran an item of "Incidental Intelligence": An executive, going through his secretary's files after hours, found in the H drawer a fat folder marked HAPPEN, POSSIBLY SOMETHING WILL. That secretary wasn't as dumb as you may think.

Next, "turn the problem around." Often a problem can be solved by looking at it upside down. A mathematician, Karl Jacobi, said that this is *the* basic formula for mathematical discoveries. I am not sure that's true; but it's certainly a technique worth trying. Are you dealing with a general rule, a proverbial truth, a basic principle? Remember what George Santayana said: "Almost every wise saying has an opposite one, no less wise, to balance it." Here's a pet example of mine. You know the saying "Never strike a child in anger"? Well, Bernard Shaw once wrote this: "If you strike a child, take care that you strike it in anger. . . . A blow in cold blood neither can nor should be forgiven."

Third, don't be afraid of the ridiculous. Alfred North Whitehead wrote: "Almost all really new ideas have a certain aspect of foolishness when they are first produced." There's a good reason for that. As you have seen, problems are often solved by looking at things in a seemingly unsuitable pattern. There's something funny about such a sudden shift of focus; in fact, surprise twists are the basic element of humor. It's downright ridiculous to compare a loan to Britain to lending a neighbor a garden hose; but that ridiculous idea solved the problem.

End of preparation stage. What follows next? Dr. Hutchinson said it best: Frustration. Remember that. When you are through with the preparation stage and frustration sets in, don't worry: it's natural. Relax and give your unconscious a chance.

To put your unconscious to work, the first rule is to give it time. As long as you're working frantically to find the solution, your unconscious doesn't have a chance. Relax; do something else; go to the movies; get some sleep.

If you have to solve a problem, turn away from it for a time and attend to some other routine matter. Above all, be sure you have time to think. Don't clutter your day with a lot of details. Spend some time by yourself—and I mean by yourself: don't be a slave to the telephone.

And don't think that problems are solved between nine and five only. The unconscious picks its own times and places. Some time ago a group of research chemists were asked when and how they got their scientific ideas. Here are some of their answers:

"While dodging automobiles across Park Row and Broadway, New York."

"Sunday in church as the preacher was announcing the text."

"At three o'clock in the morning."

"In the evening when alone in the study room."

"In the morning when shaving."

"In the early morning while in bed."

"Just before and just after an attack of gout."

"Late at night after working intensively for some hours."

"Invariably at night after retiring for sleep."

"In the plant one Sunday morning about 9 A.M. when no one was around."

"While riding in a very early train to another city."

"While resting and loafing on the beach."

"While sitting at my desk doing nothing, and thinking about other matters."

"After a month's vacation, as I was dressing after a bath in the sea."

The classic statement on the matter was made in 1891 by the German physicist Helmholtz at a banquet on his seventieth birthday:

After investigating a problem in all directions, happy ideas come unexpectedly, without effort, like an inspiration. So far as I am concerned, they have never come to me when my mind was fatigued, or when I was at my working table. . . . They came particularly readily during the slow ascent of wooded hills on a sunny day.

A charming picture—but wooded hills on sunny days are hard to come by in modern life. Sleep at night, on the other hand, is available to us all. And there we run into a question. Some of those chemists got their ideas in the evening, some others in the morning. Which is the better time for producing ideas?

A surprising answer to this question comes from Dr. Nathaniel Kleitman of the University of Chicago. Dr. Kleitman found that everybody runs through a daily cycle of rising and falling temperature; the mind is creative when our temperature curve is up and sluggish when it is down. People, Dr. Kleitman says, fall in three groups: the morning types who hit their mental stride in the morning, the evening types who are at their best late in the afternoon, and the lucky morning-and-evening types, who have a level high temperature "plateau" from morning till evening. If you hate to get up in the morning, chances are your mind will sparkle in the evening; if you are a washout at a late bridge game, you may be a champion problem-solver at 6 A.M.

Even if you know what type you are, you can't always arrange your life and work accordingly. But you can do certain things. If you are a morning type, don't spend the first half of your day with dull routine and try to be creative in the afternoon; if you are an evening type, defer productive work till the end of the day.

Professional writers often furnish good examples of thinker's schedules. Here are a few:

Ernest Hemingway: "The earliest part of the morning is the best for me. I wake always at first light and get up and start working."

John O'Hara: "My working time is late at night. Evenings I'd go and sit around drinking coffee and talking to people until about midnight, then go back to my room and write . . . Usually I kept going until about seven o'clock."

Helen MacInnes: "After dark I start some music I like, sit on the living room couch with a pad and pencil and write a chapter."

Katharine Brush: "I start at eight each morning and work through lunch until two-thirty or so. Then I knock off for the afternoon and often work again in the evening. If I'm not going to work in the evening, I keep at it longer in the afternoon."

Arnold Toynbee, the British historian: "I write every morning, whether I am in the mood or not. I sit down to write straightaway after breakfast, before dealing with my correspondence or any other business, and I do this writing at home. Then I go for lunch to the Royal Institute of International Affairs, and, in my office there, from after lunch till 6:45, dictate my letters, see people, do my work in editing the Institute's political history of the war, and do my writing for this history as well. In fact, I give half my day to one job and half to another, and find refreshment in switching my mind to and fro in this way."

Claude G. Bowers, the biographer-diplomat: "I prefer the smallest room I can find for my work and artificial light, finding this shuts out the present and makes for concentration. . . . *Jefferson and Hamilton,*

The Tragic Era, and the Beveridge were written at night while writing editorials for *The Evening World* by day. Dinner at 5:30 and from 6 to 11 I shut myself in my cubbyhole. . . . During seventeen years as Ambassador in Spain and Chile I have found time to write by avoiding bridge and golf."

With these writers, we have passed through the preparation, frustration and relaxation stages, and have arrived at the stage of creation. Once the idea is born, tips are unnecessary—except one: *write it down.* The best idea is useless if it is lost and forgotten. Catch your ideas alive. Keep a notebook handy; if you don't have a notebook, find a pad; if you can't find a pad, use an old envelope. But don't let the idea get away. It may never come back.

I started this chapter with a list of reminders. I'll end it with a list of tips:

1. Write the problem down.

2. Translate the problem into plain English.

3. If possible, translate the problem into figures, mathematical symbols or graphs.

4. Don't rely on your memory but use written or printed sources.

5. Know how to use a library.

6. Take notes and keep files.

7. Discuss the problem with others.

8. Use a check list of categories, adding new ones from time to time.

9. Try turning the problem upside down.

10. Don't be afraid of the ridiculous.

11. If you feel frustrated, don't worry. Relax; turn to other work; rest; sleep.

12. Take time to be by yourself. Free yourself of trivial work. Shut out interruptions.

13. Know the time of day when your mind works best and arrange your schedule accordingly.

14. When you get an idea, write it down.

CHAPTER 18

The Three R's—a Refresher Course

Desultory reading has always been my greatest pleasure.

—G. C. Lichtenberg

The title of this chapter is meant literally. Of the fourteen tips on thinking you just read, seven have to do with Reading, 'Riting, and 'Rithmetic. That's why I think a "Three R's Refresher Course" belongs in this book.

Most of my brief course will deal with the First R—Reading. Or rather, it will deal with the kind of reading you do for the immediate purpose of thinking—collecting information, gathering data, doing research. But before I go into all that, let me say this: The other kind of reading—reading for fun—is just as important. Lots of people, including Schopenhauer, have said that aimless reading is bad for thinking. Nonsense. You can't think without a store of ideas and you never can tell when and how your casual reading will come in handy.

This book, for instance, includes references to *The Just and the Unjust* by James Gould Cozzens (which I once borrowed from a friend), *The Way of an Investigator* by Walter B. Cannon (which I picked out of the box in front of a secondhand bookstore) and *Mechanization Takes Command* by Siegfried Giedion (which I dipped into before giving it to my brother-in-law for Christmas). And the motto for this chapter is by the eighteenth-century German writer Lichtenberg, whose wonderful *Reflections* I discovered twenty years ago. So my first tip on reading is simply this: Be a reader. Read anything and everything, the more the better. Keep a book on the fire of your mind all the time. Follow your fancy. Read books you like. Then, for a change, read a book you don't like—you may stumble into a new world.

And now let's go into the prosaic business of how to read for a purpose.

If you are like most Americans, your reading ability is pretty poor. I hasten to add that this isn't your fault: you just weren't taught properly at school. Chances are, you started in first grade with what's called the recognition method of learning to read. That method is wrong, foolish and completely unscientific.

You don't have to accept this on my say-so. Language scholars are unanimous about it. The greatest of them, the late Leonard Bloomfield, wrote: "Our schools are utterly benighted in linguistic matters. . . . Their methods of teaching children to read are devised by schoolmen who do not know the relation of writing to language. The result is that years of every child's time are wasted; we actually have 'remedial reading' classes in our high schools." Before he died, Bloomfield wrote a primer based on scientific principles; but the recognition method is so firmly entrenched in our schools that nobody has ever dared to publish it. The whole matter amounts to one of our greatest educational scandals.

Unfortunately, there's little you can do about it. If you have small children, they may yet learn to read properly; but you yourself will have to mend and fix your own reading skill as best you can.

"Remedial reading" experts come in two varieties: the speeder-uppers and the slower-downers. A typical speeder-upper is Mr. Norman Lewis, author of *How to Read Better and Faster*; a well-known slower-downer is Mr. Mortimer J. Adler, author of *How to Read a Book*. Both groups, it seems, have got *something*.

The speeder-uppers start with the undeniable fact that fast readers are better readers than slow ones. If you're average, your reading rate is about two hundred words per minute. Learn how to read four hundred words a minute, and you'll be able to get the same amount of information in half the time—just move your eyes twice as fast along the printed lines. Or so the speeder-uppers seem to think—forgetting that reading at double speed may be only half as effective. Today all educational centers use machines to speed up readers' eye movements; yet, a recent survey came to the sad conclusion that "there is really no evidence to support the view that eye movements determine reading proficiency."

The solution seems to be to speed up reading *indirectly*; try to be faster in picking up meaning, and your eyes will move in a swifter rhythm. To do that, focus on essentials; go easy on unessentials; try not to see conjunctions, prepositions, and articles, the small change of language. Force yourself to go as fast as you can; experiment with less than comfortable speed.

And what do the slower-downers have to offer? Mr. Adler tells you that you should read each book three times—but, he says, an expert reader can do these three readings at the same time. The first reading is "structural": look at the structure of the book, find out what the author is trying to do and how. The second reading is "interpretative": go ahead and read, word for word. The third reading is "critical": think about what you have read.

The most valuable idea here seems to be the "first reading"—or let's call it "prereading." If you want to be a good reader, get a general notion of the structure and purpose of what you're about to read before you start.

My advice to you is a compromise between the two schools of thought: Go slow in preparing your mind for what you're going to read; then go fast during the actual reading. In addition, if you read to get ideas, make sure you can refer back to what you've read.

The most common sources of information, of course, are newspaper items, magazine articles, reports and books. Here are some tips on how to read them.

To read newspapers, know the "inverted-pyramid" formula. Most news reports—not all of them but most—are written like this: First comes the solid base of the "pyramid," telling the climax of the story. Then comes the rest of the pyramid down to the tip, with details of decreasing importance and interest. Next, if there is space left, comes a second pyramid, starting with the base—the climax of the story over again—followed again by details of less and less interest. After that, if there's still more room, comes a third pyramid, again starting with the same climax, and again petering out into minor details.

This sounds odd, but open your paper and you'll find I am right. Take a random example (I have shown the three inverted pyramids by putting the three "bases" in boldface type, shading off into italics and roman type):

TRAIN HITS VIRGINIA SCHOOL BUS; 5 PUPILS DIE, 39 OTHERS ESCAPE

Farmville, Va., March 13 (AP)—A passenger train struck

the rear of a crowded school bus at a grade crossing west of here late today, killing five children and injuring at least ten others.

Attendants at Southside Community Hospital said a preliminary examination showed only one child hurt seriously.

There were 44 children aboard the bus. It was hit shortly after 4 p.m. at the Elam crossing, 14 miles west of here along U.S. Route 460.

Witnesses said the train apparently hit the back section of the bus, shearing off a fourth of the vehicle. The rear end shattered into three or four pieces.

Bits of wreckage were scattered from 30 to 50 yards along the main line of the Norfolk and Western Railway between Roanoke and Norfolk. The main part of the bus, however, stood at the crossing where it was hit.

State Police Sgt. L. L. Stanley quoted the bus driver, John Oscar Robinson, as saying he did not see the train coming. Mr. Robinson said he started to cross the tracks and then felt the collision, Sgt. Stanley said.

The dead and injured were in the rear section of the vehicle, state police said. Names were withheld pending a complete check of their identity.

Prince Edward County school authorities said the bus was carrying children home from a high school and elementary school in Farmville.

As you see, the story is told three times; the collision happens in the first paragraph, then again in the third, and then again in the sixth. On top of it all, it is also told in the headline.

If you want to be a good newspaper reader, you have to learn inverted-pyramid reading. If all you want to know is in the headline, read just the headline; if it's the first pyramid, read that and stop; if you feel like reading two pyramids, read two, focusing on the lead paragraph and reading on with less and less attention. Adapt the rhythm of your reading to the rhythm of the writing.

Many newspaper stories begin on page one and, after a paragraph or two, "jump" to page seventeen or twenty-nine or whatever. If the whole story is important to you, resist the temptation to let it jump away from you for good. Turn to page seventeen and finish it.

If the story is worth remembering, clip it. Ever so often I see a man on the commuter's train rip something out of his paper and put it in his pocket. That's a better picture of a thinker than Rodin's naked brooder.

Next, learn how to read magazine articles. Again, adapt your reading rhythm to the writing rhythm. Typically, a popular magazine article is written on the sandwich or layer-cake principle—alternating between layers of information and layers of entertainment. If you read for ideas, focus sharply on the factual stuff and take in the anecdotes and illustrations with a casual glance or two. (This isn't easy; in a skillfully written piece, the temptation is to read just the other way round.)

To use a magazine article for reference, clip it and file it. If it isn't your own copy, note the volume, date and page.

When you get to reading reports and scientific papers, you're better off. They are *built* for efficient reading. A properly written report or paper winds up with a neat summary saying everything important in a nutshell. So the expert report reader immediately turns to the last page, reads the summary, and that's that. Only if he needs to know more, does he go back to the beginning. If a scientist wants a paper for reference, he gets a copy and files it. You too can get a copy of any scientific paper you want by simply writing the author for a reprint. If he hasn't run out of copies, he'll send you one with his compliments.

Finally, here is how to read a book (for a purpose, that is). Books are not written by any general formula; they are built any which way. To find out about a book's structure, start by slowly reading *everything but* the main text. Start with the front cover, the back cover, the two jacket flaps; then work your way through the title page, the dedication, the preface, the foreword, the introduction and the acknowledgments; then go through the table of contents with a fine-tooth comb. By the time you've done all this, you're ready for page one: you'll know, in a general way, who the author is, what he is trying to do, how he is trying to do it, and what comes first, second, and third. If you still don't, leaf slowly through the book, dipping in to read a bit here and there. Don't start reading the book without knowing what you can look forward to.

After you are through with a book, be sure you can use the ideas in it for reference. At this point, let me quote the British writer-diplomat Harold Nicolson, who was asked to advise a graduating class:

My advice is to go to France, direct from New York to Cherbourg and to remain there for at least three months, if possible living in a French family. My second piece of advice is always to mark your books and write a personal index for yourself on the flyleaf.

I'm not sure about the first piece of advice, but the second is perfect. Of course, if you use a library book, you can't write in the book but have to take notes; if you own the book, however, follow Nicolson's advice to the letter. In other words, never read a book without keeping a pencil handy. (To start you off on the personal-index habit, I have reserved page 204 of this book for "Your Personal Index." There are a few printed items as a starter; take a pencil and go on from there.)

And that ends our discussion of the First R. We'll deal with the Second R, 'Riting, in a jiffy, leaving to one side the whole matter of writing as communication. Let's concentrate simply on writing as a tool for note-taking.

If you know shorthand, you're way ahead of the rest of mankind as a note-taker. If you don't, use a "notehand."

There are any number of systems, but my suggestion is that you work out your own. Here are some tips:

1. Make use of common or "natural" abbreviations, like 1, 2 (two, to, too), 4 (four, for), 1st, 2d, 3d, &, #, ½, %, b (be), q (question), r (are), u (you), biz (business), dif (difference), pix (pictures).

2. Adopt a system of letters for common articles, prepositions, pronouns and conjunctions like t (the), tt (that), o (of), f (from), w (with), xc (except).

3. Abbreviate suffixes, like n (ion, ation, ition), v (ive, ative), l (al, ical, ogical), mt (ment).

4. Abbreviate all words by writing the essential letters only, particularly leaving out vowels. For instance: "Abbr al wds by wrtg t essl ltrs onl, pticly lvg ou vwls."

And that ends what I have to say here about the Second R. Now to the Third R—'Rithmetic.

Let's start with the fact that practically all the mathematics you learned in school is of no use to you today. Algebra, geometry, trigonometry—you hardly remember what it was all about. Arithmetic, though, does come up sometimes in your life, and you wish you remembered it a little better.

My first piece of advice here is very simple. If you have a lot of figuring to do, don't try to do it all with your rusty school arithmetic. If a lot of addition comes your way, get an adding machine; if it's multiplication, get a slide rule and take a day to learn how to use it. Just face the fact that your mind shook off mathematics as a dog shakes off water, and act accordingly.

For what's left of arithmetic, use shortcuts. Here are a few:

1. If round figures will do, use round figures. To add $12.95, $6.20, and $3.98, say, "13, 6, and 4 are 23" and let it go at that. When you need the exact sum, you can always add it up to $23.13.

2. To add a column of figures, look for pairs that add up to 10.

Example:

18	
93	
67	
24	
22	
96	
320	

In adding, group $8 + 2$, $3 + 7$, $4 + 6$, $1 + 9$, $6 + 2 + 2$, and save time.

3. Don't forget to cancel fractions. When you multiply $5/16$ by $4/10$, cancel first the 5's and the 4's. Result: $1/8$. (Saves you the detour of $20/160$.)

4. To multiply by 25, add two zeros and divide by 4.

5. "Cross-multiply" two-digit numbers. Example:

$$\begin{array}{r} 29 \\ 67 \\ \hline 1943 \end{array}$$

Do this as follows: "Seven times 9 is 63; write 3, carry 6. Six times 9 is 54 and 7 times 2 is 14; 54 and 14 is 68; plus 6 carryover is 74; write 4, carry 7; 6 times 2 is 12, plus 7 carryover is 19." Product: 1943.

6. To multiply figures with decimals, think of how many decimals you'll want in the product and round off to the needed number of decimals *before* you multiply. Example: You want to multiply $17.38 by 6.85, to get a product in dollars and cents. To save steps, multiply 17.4 by 6.8. Result: $118.32. (The long way, the result would be $119.05; the 73¢ difference may not be worth the extra effort.)

End of the Third R Refresher—almost, but not quite. When it comes to statistics, you're up against something you were never taught in school. Nevertheless, you have to read and understand statistics every day. Here are a few elementary things about it you ought to know.

Statistics mainly come in the form of averages. The first and most important point about averages is the fact that they are often wrong. Writers have a way of referring to the typical or average case without paying the slightest attention to actual facts. For instance, you've heard and read a thousand times that the average American family lives in a small town. Actually, as I have mentioned before, 56 per cent of our population live in metropolitan areas; another 36 per cent, according to the 1950 census, are rural. This leaves 8 per cent small-town Americans—hardly typical for the country as a whole, you'll admit.

As to the "typical" family, I quote the following bit from a recent magazine article:

Let us look in for a moment at a typical American family. It is a rainy Saturday afternoon and they are all at home. The twins are stretched on the floor, tinkering with an electric train; Judy is curling her hair by the kitchen mirror; and her mother is putting a cake in the oven. When they hear father's car, they all run to the door . . .

Twins, my eye! There's one twin birth in ninety-five.

Some averages, though, are right as rain but utterly meaningless. I've collected a few of those. If you are an average American, for instance, you have four defective teeth and three dollars worth of gold in your mouth and consume each year one hundred bottles of soft drinks, sixteen lollypops, and two ounces of snuff. If you are a woman, you have one chance in 2,094.2 to get a mink coat this year.

The last figure brings up the question of the spurious decimal. To use an impressive figure, I'd estimate that about 74.893 per cent of all statistical decimals are useful only for conveying the impression of immense accuracy. Last year a survey of New York City College students showed that male students shaved 4.7 times a week. Figure out for yourself how they did it.

Finally, there is the awkward fact that averages come in three assorted types: the mean, the median and the mode. In most situations they are *not* the same. Far from it. There is a world of a difference between them.

The mean is what you get when you divide the total by the number of cases; the median is the midpoint between the upper and lower halves. Let me illustrate with the 1948 income statistics of U. S. lawyers. There were 140,000 of them engaged in independent practice; their mean income was $8,121. Their *median* income was $5,719. Some reasons for the $2,400 difference: Seven out of ten independent lawyers served mainly individuals rather than business firms; three-fourths of them,

practiced alone, without partners; lawyers in places under 1,000 population earned only about $3,700, those in firms with nine or more members
averaged $27,000.

In most statistics you're interested in, the median tells the story better
than the mean. Yet most averages you see are means. Watch out for that
difference—make an effort to find out about the median.

Then there is the mode—the case that occurs most often. Dr. L. Susan
Stebbing, the logician, thought that in popular speech the average
usually means the mode. She was right. Average, to you, is the thing
you're apt to run into. But modes are harder to figure than means and
medians and so they are hard to come by. The mode is best but you'll
have to be satisfied with the median if you can get it.

Nowadays it is fashionable, of course, not to use figures but charts
and graphs. Chart-and-graph reading, too, is part of the Three R's and
a very important one at that. The basic rule is simple: *Don't go by what
you see.*

Sounds like a paradox? Not at all. The same set of figures may be
presented in a dozen different graphs, giving a dozen different impressions. A straight line in one chart may appear as a curve in another, a
steep rise here may correspond to a flat plateau there, a wide gap on one
graph may be an imperceptible difference on another. Graphs and charts
are, by their very nature, little bundles of optical illusions. Some are
more so and some less, but the principle holds. Therefore: Don't go by
what you see.

Instead, go by what you read. Read the caption, the accompanying
text, everything that gives you a clue as to what the graph is supposed
to show. Reading visual materials is like reading anything else: you
have to start reading with a careful *prereading.*

I'll use two maps to make this point clear. They are both maps of
Manhattan Island; both were prepared by the Hagstrom Company of
New York. Yet on the first, Manhattan looks half as wide as on the
second. Why? Because neither map is supposed to show what Manhattan
is actually like. The first is *Hagstrom's Map How to Get In and Out of
New York by Automobile,* while the second is designed to show the
New York City Transit System: Subway and Elevated Lines. Both are
excellent maps for their specific purposes; but don't go by what you see
on either to guess the width of Manhattan.

And that definitely winds up my Three R's Refresher Course.

Thanks for sticking around till the end. Class dismissed.

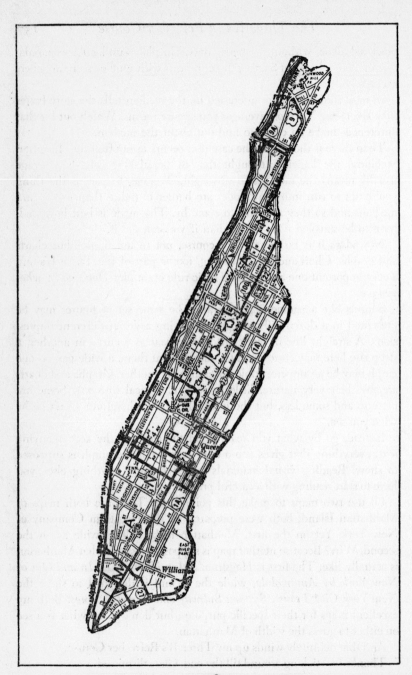

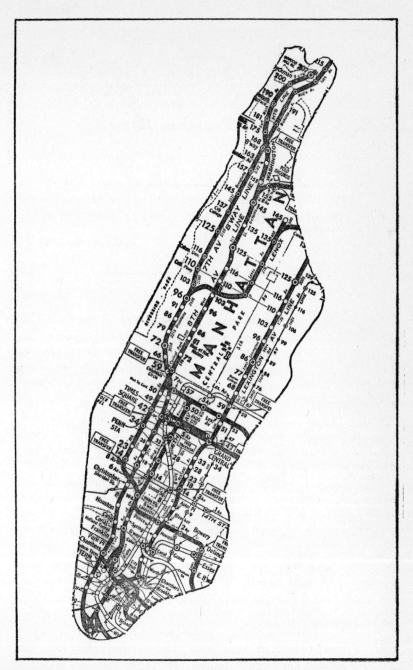

CHAPTER 19

Thinking Begins at Home

When men and women agree, it is only in their conclusions; their reasons are always different.

—George Santayana

A family, in Ogden Nash's classic definition, is "a unit composed not only of children, but of men, women, an occasional animal, and the common cold." Is it a good place to think? Yes and no. If you want to shut out noise and interruptions, you'd better go someplace else. But if you want to pool quickly the viewpoints of various ages and sexes, stay right at home.

The basis of clear thinking, as I said at the beginning of this book, is the realization that we think with our experience. The family—a mixed assortment of all kinds and degrees of experience—is the place to learn this once and for all.

Take the main family problem—bringing up children. In dealing with a child, the first thing you have to realize is that he or she doesn't have your experience. There's no point in assuming that a child's mind is furnished with the same concepts as yours: it just isn't. It takes the child years to acquire all those ideas that make up an adult's physical, social, and moral world; in fact, the process is a definition of mentally growing up. Promise a small child something for "day after tomorrow" and you'll find that he is vague about what you meant; give him a dime for two nickels and you'll find that, to him, it's not a fair exchange.

The French psychologist Piaget spent most of his life tracing step by step the growth of ideas in young minds. Our American child specialists have applied such knowledge practically. Books like those by Dr. Arnold

160

Gesell of Yale represent perfectly the intelligent adult attitude toward children. They are full of wise insights into children's minds like these:

If a five-year-old does something he should not do or did not want or mean to do, he is likely to blame the nearest person. If his mother is close by, the child may accuse her with a "Look what you made me do." A sibling, a dog or another child may be blamed when they are part of the scene of action. There may be more validity to this accusation than one at first realizes. When a child is running down a hill and meets another child, there is no doubt that he may show an unsteadiness in his running and finally fall. The other child did not push him, but the other child's presence did remove his attention from his running. . . .

An eight-year-old is not prone to take the property of others. However, with his awareness of money and what it can buy, he may be found taking some of the household supply of money. This is usually considered by parents as a far greater offense than taking pencils and erasers at an earlier age. But the child is in each case expressing a need characteristic of his age. Parents should be aware of these needs and should see that they are provided for in suitable ways. . . .

It is not always easy to think of the world as it looks through five- or eight-year-old eyes, and parents can never be perfect, even with the aid of books like those by Gesell. But they can, as far as possible, hang on to the basic principle: Try to look at the situation from the child's point of view.

And what about the care and feeding of husbands and wives? The same principle holds. Husbands' and wives' viewpoints are never the same, and the secret of a happy marriage is mutual understanding that they aren't.

There's some interesting scientific evidence for the fact that men and women think in different ways. The "embedded-figures" test on pages 94 to 98, for instance (which is related to administrative ability) usually takes women longer than men. Tests like Dr. Duncker's box problem on page 92 are also harder for women than for men. On the other hand, girls are generally superior to boys in verbal facility and languages (which are related to mental flexibility). All of which seems to show that when it comes to problem-solving, men are better at analyzing situations but women are better at shifting to new mental patterns. (Let's by-pass here the question of whether this difference is "natural" or "cultural"; whatever the reason, it exists.)

The difference is beautifully illustrated by a recent Perry Barlow cartoon in *The New Yorker*. "Now, no fair *thinking!*" the wife says to her husband across the checkers board, and this of course is an extremely funny thing to say. Yet, on second thought, maybe it isn't so absurd after all. Remember Wertheimer's two boys playing badminton? Is it fair for a husband to *think* during a family game of checkers? Considering the circumstances, it may well be that it isn't. Matrimonial checkers isn't played to win but to spend a quiet evening at home.

It is natural for Mr. Barlow, as a man, to use female lack of logic as a source of humor. But the scatterbrained little woman has become a stereotype even among women. Miss Bj Kidd, a life-insurance expert, describes at length female helplessness in the face of such things as insurance policies, checkbook balances and $3.98 price tags; and Miss Emily Kimbrough tells the following story about a checking account she had as a young girl:

When she closed the account, the teller asked: "Why is it that over the years, ever so often, you've made out checks to cash or to self for the most peculiar amounts—$1.89, $2.13—sums like that?"

To which Miss Kimbrough answered: "Why, I don't see anything peculiar in that. I write them when my balance gets into odd numbers which are hard to subtract, especially nines. I do one check that brings my balance to zeros and round numbers again so that I can make a fresh start."

Well, it seems fair to assume that in general women don't make as good bank tellers or actuaries as men. Most people would agree with that statement. What they usually don't realize is that in certain types of mental work women may do better than men.

How do women perform on juries, for instance? According to a recent *New York Times* article, judges, lawyers, and jury officials agree that "since women have fewer commercial prejudices and intellectual calluses, they make fewer prejudicial judgments."

Or how about women lawyers? I quote Judge Jerome Frank:

Women lawyers effectively employ in court-rooms and law offices the insights women have traditionally used as wives and mothers in making life livable for their men, who tend too frequently to use overprecise abstractions. . . . Women usually have a way of piercing to the core of the matter. . . . The modern woman lawyer understands that law is not a science but an art, the art of intelligent compromise. . . .

In the courts, as in the home [Judge Frank continues], allowances must be made for extenuating circumstances, specific cases must be individualized.

This gives us a clue to what makes for good thinking in a home. There should be teamwork, and there should be a general division of labor: let husbands attend to basic rules and wives take care of compromises and exceptions.

In many American homes, husband and wife lean over backward in "minding their own business": he goes to the office and she takes care of the house and the children. And yet, a good part of his work may be in human relations which she understands better than he does; and in many of her time-schedule and consumer problems she could profit from his advice. Husband-and-wife thinking means, first of all, putting their heads *together*.

Family teamwork in thinking is common when it comes to big decisions like buying a new house. This is where husbands, wives and older children get together discussing the problem, weighing the pros and cons of possible solutions, planning with pencil and paper, and surveying the available factual information. There are other big occasions: shifting to another school, planning vacations, buying a new car.

On the whole, however, the main trouble with family thinking is that there isn't enough of it going on. For one thing, we don't always realize that negative decisions are just as important as positive ones. We spend a lot of time thinking about moving to another house but never look into the question whether it's wise to stay where we are. The great danger to clear thinking is inertia: family affairs, like business, need something like an annual inventory, balance sheet and review of progress. Most people realize today that they should have an annual physical checkup (although they don't always act on that realization); but few take time out for an annual occupational, educational, social or emotional checkup. Economically, we all have to do that sort of thing around March 15; we should have similar dates for all other aspects of our lives.

As to the minor decisions of everyday life, we hardly think about them at all. When Junior needs a new pair of shoes, we go to the store and buy him shoes; when we feel like going to the movies, we go down to the Strand. A little thought might reveal that Junior would get more out of boots and we would get more out of the British picture at the Palace; but we don't bother to think.

At Christmas, we give Aunt Emma a poinsettia because we've always given Aunt Emma a poinsettia at Christmas. If we considered the matter as a problem to be solved by thinking, we might discover that a repetitive poinsettia doesn't make a good Christmas present to anybody; besides, a quick glance at Aunt Emma would make it clear that she isn't the poinsettia-loving type. Of course, her name is Emma and she is an old maid; but let's remember that in clear thinking we have to get away from word labels and conventional ideas and look at the actual facts. Aunt Emma, it so happens, is not at all the thin, genteel spinster type. She is fat, jolly, bustling with energy, and remarkably efficient at her job. She has no time for flowers and no interest in them. She is a chain smoker and loves to drive around in her old, rattletrap car. She loves children and is especially fond of her youngest niece.

If we'd tackle the Christmas-present-for-Aunt-Emma problem with a check list like the one on page 119, we might arrive at a new approach. The list raises the question of giving two presents instead of one. Why not? There's no rule that says Christmas presents have to be in the singular. Let's give Aunt Emma two, one that'll especially suit her daily life and one that shows our sentiments. Together, they'll still cost less than that annual poinsettia. Let's give her a gadget for lighting cigarettes in her car and a snapshot of our younger daughter in a dimestore frame.

Trivial? Of course. But most of our life is made up of trivial things. Let's give them a little more thought and we'll have improved the basic fabric of our life.

In short, let's do more thinking right at home. Let's look around: Is our home equipped for thinking? Thinking needs tools; do we have them handy?

I know what you're thinking of now, but you misunderstand me: I don't mean those bookshelves in your living room. Sure, I am all for having a lot of books, and I hope that you have a nice collection of classics and best sellers. But I'm not talking about those right now. How well equipped is the *reference section* of your private library?

I take it that you have a good dictionary and I hope you have an encyclopedia. While these are relatively expensive, the rest of your thinking equipment is cheap:

Do you own a *World Almanac* (or *Information Please Almanac*)? If not, get one. You'll be amazed at the fantastic range of information covered.

Do you have a first-aid manual? A book on child care? A cookbook? A book on household repairs? A garden book? There are many excellent examples of each. Some of the best are available for practically nothing from the federal government. (Write to the Superintendent of Documents, Government Printing Office, Washington 25, D. C.; while you're at it, ask for literature on other subjects you're interested in.)

What newspapers and magazines do you subscribe to? They are as essential for your private affairs as scientific journals are for the work of a scientist. Clip those articles about new drugs; hang on to those newspaper items about taxes and insurance.

Above all, don't read just one newspaper or magazine. To keep your mind in shape, keep it exposed to different viewpoints. I grew up in a house that had a conservative *and* a liberal paper on the breakfast table and can testify to the fact that there's no better tonic for family thinking. If you don't care to take two papers, use magazines to keep posted on what the other half thinks; or at least make a point of listening regularly to commentators you don't agree with.

There's no point in clipping newspapers or magazines if you don't keep files. Files don't have to be elaborate; but you should have them and keep them ready for use. You should have a place for important documents, like insurance policies, mortgages, deeds, birth and marriage certificates, and your will; if you keep them in your bank, you should have records of them at home. You should have a businesslike way with your checkbook; and you should have a memo pad, up-to-date maps and timetables, an up-to-date address book, and a diary for important dates and appointments.

Last but not least, you should have a typewriter so that you can make and keep carbon copies of important outgoing letters.

Disgusted with these suggestions? Do you feel I am trying to turn your home into an office and reduce everything to business routine?

Up to a point, I am. I think the average home could profit from a lot more office routine. On the other hand, as you'll see in a minute, I think there's far too much of it in the average business.

C H A P T E R   2 0

The Mind from Nine to Five

Few people do business well who do nothing else.
—Lord Chesterfield

On February 3, 1951, at a dinner at the Waldorf-Astoria Hotel, Mr. Herman Ackman received a $1,000 award for having negotiated "the most ingenious realty transaction in Manhattan during 1950."

This is how Mr. Ackman won the $1,000: In 1942 his brokerage firm took charge of an abandoned lot on West 79th Street for $5 a month. The lot was seventy feet from the corner of Riverside Drive. The Seamen's Bank of Savings held a mortgage on it. There were four old houses on that corner, all belonging to different owners.

Mr. Ackman looked at the corner with the four old houses and the abandoned lot and saw in his mind a tall modern apartment house with a river view. He set to work negotiating the assembling of the corner, the financing, and the eventual building. After eight years the first tenants moved in. The whole deal, as was said at the award dinner, "ran the gamut of enthusiasm, expectation, frustration, reawakening of interest, heartache, renewed hope and then—after plans and programs underwent various changes—final consummation."

Business transactions are not often described in such terms. Read the words over and you'll find that they could just as well refer to writing a novel, fighting a battle or courting a girl. "Was ever woman in this humor woo'd?" Is this the way businessmen spend their day at the office?

Quite often, the answer is yes. Of course, business isn't all like that, full of adventure and strong emotion. But neither is it all adding and subtracting, keeping books in order, and greeting customers with a smile.

Lately, psychologists have analyzed the kind of thinking that goes on in business, particularly the quality of mind that marks good executives. Here is what one of them found after studying closely over a hundred successful businessmen:

> Successful executives are strongly oriented to immediate realities and their implications. They are directly interested in the practical, the immediate, and the direct. . . . They have the ability to take several seemingly isolated events or facts and to see relationships that exist between them. Further, they are interested in looking into the future and are concerned with predicting the outcome of their decisions and actions. . . .
>
> Decisiveness is a further trait . . . an ability to come to a decision among several alternative courses of action. . . . Very seldom does this ability fail.

The late Lord Tweedsmuir (John Buchan), governor-general of Canada, learned the art of administration under Lord Milner, the famous administrator of South Africa. In his autobiography, Tweedsmuir poses the question: "In what precisely lay Milner's administrative genius?" He answers it in much the same way as the psychologist just quoted:

> In the first place, he had in a high degree what Cavour called the *"tact des choses possibles."* The drawback to a completely rational mind is that it is apt to assume that what is flawless in logic is therefore practicable. Milner never made that mistake; he knew too well the stubborn illogicality of facts. But he seemed to have an instinct for what was possible. . . .
>
> Milner had the power of divining the item on which everything hung. He could do what the lumberman does in a log-jam, and pick out the key log which, once moved, sets the rest going. . . .
>
> But his greatest administrative gift was his courage. He had what the French know as *courage de tête*, the boldness to trust his reason. When he had satisfied himself about a particular course—and he took long to satisfy—his mind seemed to lock down on it, and after that there was no going back. Doubts were done with, faced and resolved; he moved with the confident freedom of a force of nature.

So here we have the three supreme qualities you need to be or become a good executive:

1. A sense of realities.
2. An eye for possibilities.
3. The ability to make up your mind.

Students of such matters are pretty well agreed that these three qualities are more important in business than knowledge of facts and figures. It never happens in business that *all* factors are known, and as long as they aren't, the businessman has to guess at realities and possibilities, and make up his mind on the basis of these guesses.

To be sure, the more facts the better, and that's why there has recently been a tremendous increase in all kinds of business research. But there's a limit to what you can do with facts and statistics. You can assemble them, do all sorts of mathematical operations, run them through adding machines, punchcard machines and electronic machines. Yet in the end, at least at the present stage, you're up against something a robot can't do but an experienced human being can.

For instance, there's the new "theory of games and economic behavior" that approaches business strategy by way of probability mathematics. The originators, John von Neumann and Oskar Morgenstern, have shown that business behavior can be analyzed mathematically after the model of a poker game. Sounds very exciting and revolutionary, but here's the catch:

> For example [Dr. Morgenstern explains], two competing automobile manufacturers may each have a large number of strategies involving the choice of various body designs, the addition of new accessories, the best times to announce new models and price changes, and so on. It has been estimated that the calculations for a game in which one manufacturer has 100 possible strategies and his competitor had 200 (a not uncommon situation) *would take about a year on an electronic computer.*

So you see, it'll be a long time until business deals can be worked automatically on a mathematical basis. Meanwhile, businessmen will have to act on guesses and hunches and, like Mr. Ackman, will have to "run the gamut of expectation, frustration, heartache, and renewed hope."

On top of all that, business thinking is complicated by the fact that business deals with people. People are unpredictable anyway, but people in groups and organizations are specially so. A good businessman has to have a sense of how people will react upon one another.

For example, there is the matter of organization charts. A good executive knows that there is no magic in a neat arrangement of boxes and lines. It's the *informal* organization that counts, the one that never appears on a chart. In February, 1951, the newspapers carried a large organization chart that had been submitted to the Senate Committee investigating the RFC. That's the kind of chart I mean. It was crisscrossed with lines labeled PERSONAL FRIENDS, HUSBAND AND WIFE, FATHER AND DAUGHTER, BROTHER-IN-LAW, CLOSE FRIENDS, and so on.

Similarly, a good executive carries in his head an organization chart labeled FATHER-IN-LAW AND SON-IN-LAW, WENT TO SAME SCHOOL, PLAY GOLF TOGETHER, IN COMPETITION FOR HIGHER JOB, COMMUTE ON SAME TRAIN or WIVES USED TO BE FRIENDS. These are the realities that make or break the effectiveness of an organization.

Then there is the subtle matter of teamwork. Ever since the surprising experiments at the Hawthorne Western Electric plant—where workers did better and better under worse and worse conditions because they got into the spirit of doing the tests as a team—researchers have been analyzing the elusive power of the *esprit de corps*. The end of these researches is not yet in sight, but we do know that working as a group has an astonishing effect on people.

The act of decision-making itself is something that seems to escape analysis. Lord Tweedsmuir, who was a literary man, used the beautiful word *courage* and let it go at that. Mr. Chester I. Barnard, who wrote a fascinating book on *The Functions of the Executive* when he was President of the New Jersey Bell Telephone Company, had this to add: "The fine art of executive decision consists in not deciding questions that are not now pertinent, in not deciding prematurely, in not making decisions that cannot be made effective, and in not making decisions that others should make."

Business thinking, as you see, is a complex affair. The work of an executive is an endless chain of problem-solving and decision-making; but not only that, the facts he has to act on are always incomplete, his decision has to be based on guesses about the future, and he has to estimate the reactions of many different people. And there's no getting away from making decisions, since making no decision is a decision too.

Basically, of course, business problem-solving is the same as any other kind: it is done by finding the strategic key factor or the unexpected new pattern. Business is full of examples of various types of creative thinking.

Creative thinking, for instance, may mean disregarding our own cultural conventions and adopting the ideas of other peoples. Consider the case of Mr. Clarence Birdseye, who started the frozen-food industry by falling back on the quick-freezing method of the Eskimos, about which he had learned in Labrador.

Or creative thinking may mean simply the realization that there's no particular virtue in doing things the way they've always been done. A neat example of this in the business world occurred one morning in the summer of 1949. It was about 6 A.M. and Mr. Louis Schwartz, a sportswear manufacturer, "was driving up Fifth Avenue in New York after a rough night," as he tells it. He noticed some twenty-five or thirty men in front of the fancy stores, washing down the sidewalks with hoses and brooms. This sight gave him an idea and he went into business with his Sidewalk Sanitation Service, a firm that contracts with stores to keep their sidewalks clean. Instead of by hand, the work is done with a mechanical scrubber. All that was necessary to start this unique business was the realization that the City Department of Sanitation doesn't clean sidewalks and that there's a better way to do it than with a broom.

As an example of getting away from the accepted connotations of words, take the case of Mr. Beverly Osborne of Oklahoma City. One day in 1936, he and his wife were out driving and stopped to eat their box lunch of fried chicken. When a piece of chicken slipped from her fingers, Mrs. Osborne muttered: "This is really eating chicken in the rough." The phrase started Mr. Osborne thinking. Within the next fourteen years, he built a national chain of 245 "Chicken in the Rough" restaurants, specializing in fried chicken without benefit of silverware. Displaying a nice sense of realities, Mr. Osborne had perceived that Americans *like* to eat chicken with their fingers, Emily Post to the contrary.

Finally, here are two beautiful examples of the technique of turning things upside down. Mr. James Webb Young, the advertising man who specializes in the technique of getting ideas, is proud of how he sold a crop of apples with hail marks on them. The apples had all been ordered in advance when hail storms put ugly brown spots on them. Mr. Young thought of a way of filling the orders without losing his customers. Each box of apples contained the following card:

> NOTE THE HAIL MARKS which appear as minor skin blemishes on some of these apples. These are proof of their growth at a high mountain altitude, where the sudden chills from mountain hailstorms which these apples receive while growing help firm their flesh and develop the fruit sugars which give them their fine flavor.

The other story is about the New York City chain of snack bars, Chock Full O' Nuts. For twenty years, Chock Full O' Nuts sold an excellent cup of coffee for a nickel. In the fall of 1950, coffee almost anywhere else had gone up to ten cents a cup. Chock Full O' Nuts decided to raise the price too. But it pacified its customers with the following ingenious sign:

> ### 10c A CUP
>
> As the price of coffee kept climbing, we kept diluting the coffee. It got down to where we were serving a watery cup of coffee. As the price of cream kept climbing, we kept adding more milk to the cream. It got down to where we were serving straight milk in our coffee.
>
> Customers were complaining. They had a perfect right to. When you order a cup of coffee now, you will get a full-bodied cup of coffee with straight pure cream in it.

All of these examples are business ideas, but you could hardly call them office ideas. The first goes back to a trip abroad years ago, the second appeared at 6 A.M. "after a rough night," the third sprang from an accidental remark on a vacation trip, the fourth, according to Mr. Young, came to him in the middle of the night, and the fifth I don't know about—but it looks like the kind of idea you get while you're shaving. Does this mean that a businessman should think about his business day and night? Dr. William E. Henry, the psychologist I quoted before, seems to think so. He likes to ask executives what they think of at quitting time. The successful ones, he says, think of problems left for the next day; the unsuccessful ones, "think of getting home fast to their family, or to a martini."

There's a certain amount of truth in this, but the emphasis is wrong. True, if you shut out all thoughts of business at five o'clock sharp you're not apt to get ahead in your job; but if you think of *nothing but* your business at all hours, you're apt to fall behind as an intelligent human being.

CHAPTER 21

Freedom from Error?

I beseech you, in the bowels of Christ, think it possible you may be mistaken.

—Oliver Cromwell

There are few things in the world that are as popular as error.

Some errors have been corrected and exposed for centuries but are as popular as ever; some others fly in the face of everyday experience but are widely believed in as gospel.

Popular errors have been listed and classified in many books; the New York Public Library has over twenty-five of them. The oldest is Sir Thomas Browne's *Vulgar Errors*, published in 1646, the latest is *The Natural History of Nonsense* by Bergen Evans, published in 1946. Quite a few of the errors dealt with by Sir Thomas Browne were still popular when Mr. Evans wrote his book three hundred years later. For example, both books discuss the misconception "that man's heart is to the left."

I have no ambition to add to the shelf of popular-error books, but you may be interested in a brief list of misconceptions I ran across myself. I'll set them down here in the time-honored style:

1. That Galileo climbed the Tower of Pisa and dropped two cannon balls of different weight to disprove Aristotle's theory that heavier bodies fall faster. (He didn't.)

2. That Voltaire said: "I don't agree with what you say, but I will defend to the death your right to say it." (He never said so. The quotation comes from a book *about* Voltaire, written in 1907.)

3. That in our legal system, the defendant is presumed to be inno-

cent until he is proved guilty, while on the European continent he is presumed to be guilty until he is proved innocent. (Wrong. European law has the presumption of innocence too; in fact, it's in the French Constitution but not in ours.)

4. That Abraham Lincoln jotted down the Gettysburg Address on the back of an old envelope while he was going to Gettysburg on the train. (On the contrary: he worked on it for weeks and made corrections in it even *after* it had been delivered.)

5. That in a game of heads or tails, the chances of the next toss depend on the previous ones. (No. The odds are always fifty-fifty; "a coin has no memory.")

6. That Mark Twain said: "Everybody talks about the weather, but nobody does anything about it." (He didn't; supposedly Charles Dudley Warner wrote it in an editorial for the Hartford *Courant* about 1890.)

7. That in World War II, the Army Air Force used color-blind men because they could detect camouflage better than others. (Untrue; in fact, experiments showed that men with normal vision did better.)

8. That Adolf Hitler's real name was Schicklgruber. (It wasn't. Schicklgruber was the maiden name of his grandmother; his father was born out of wedlock, but legitimized as Hitler.)

I rather expect most or all of these popular errors to be part of your mental equipment; it would be surprising if they weren't. Practically everybody believes these things. More than that: people take special pride in their misinformation. *Life* magazine recently ran a little test entitled "Are You Educated?" and included familiarity with that old story about Galileo as part of the test. A New York newspaper uses that pseudo-Voltaire quotation as the daily motto on its editorial page. A recent book on law for laymen solemnly expounds that myth about "our" presumption of innocence. The book *Mark Twain at Your Fingertips* lists the remark about the weather as a genuine saying by Mark Twain.

Why is error so popular? Even my brief list shows clearly some of the reasons.

In the first place, error is often more attractive than truth. Real life is apt to be a drab, humdrum, unglamorous business; but things-that-aren't-so are usually spectacularly exciting and fill us with a tingling sense of wonder and awe. Galileo disproving Aristotle on the Tower of Pisa—Lincoln writing his speech on the train to Gettysburg: Why, can these things have actually happened? we ask—and then believe them even more strongly just *because* they seem unbelievable. Not so long ago, Mr. Immanuel Velikovsky wrote a book in which he "proved scientifically" that the sun stood still at Jericho and that scores of other Biblical miracles actually happened. Scientists enjoyed a hearty laugh, but the general public made the book a leading best seller of 1950.

Another thing that makes error popular is that we like life to be nice and simple. Of course, life isn't like that; it's complex, irregular, hard to understand, and generally a messy thing to deal with. But error has a wonderful neatness. The laws of probability are hard to grasp, but anybody can understand that the chances of tails coming up next are better when heads have come up ten times. This is utterly wrong, to be sure; but isn't it wonderful how it simplifies things?

A third reason for our wrong beliefs goes deeper. We believe what is *comfortable* to believe. If problems are troublesome, there *must* be an easy solution; if we are worried, there *must* be something that will make us feel good. This, I think, is at the bottom of the last two on my little list of errors. To be color-blind makes you feel inferior; so there *must* be some situation where it turns out to be a good thing after all. Adolf Hitler was painful to live with on the same planet; so people derived whatever comfort there was from pinning on him the ridiculous label Schicklgruber.

The search for comfort in our worries and troubles produced the second great best seller of 1950: *Dianetics* by L. Ron Hubbard. Like *Worlds in Collision* by Velikovsky, *Dianetics* was denounced by all scientists. But since it promised an easy cure for all our mental ills, thousands and thousands of people ate it up.

Dianetics, in fact, was only one in a long line of "comfort" books— the literature on how to relax and not to worry about anything. These books are commonly classified as nonfiction books, but that doesn't mean they are factual. People read them regardless of whether they contain information or misinformation, or how much of either; they take them as sedatives.

Some years ago, Dr. Lee R. Steiner wrote a disturbing book about all this, called *Where Do People Take Their Troubles?* It presented a fantastic gallery of phony advisers people go to. Rather than think through their own problems, millions of Americans consult astrologers, graphologists, advice-to-the-lovelorn columnists, spiritualists, radio counselors, numerologists, palmists, New Thought practitioners and yoga teachers.

In other words, error is popular because people are afraid to grow up. Clear thinking means facing the fact that life is full of difficult problems, that we cannot escape from pain, discomfort and uncertainty, that we cannot attain happiness by turning away from reality. As Sigmund Freud said, we need "education to reality." Once we have had it, we "will be in the same position as the child who has left the home where he was so warm and comfortable. But, after all, is it not the destiny of childishness to be overcome? Man cannot remain a child forever; he must venture at last into the hostile world."

Even if we are willing to face reality and tackle our problems by thinking, we're up against the plain fact that thinking is hard. Sydney Smith said: "I never could find any man who could think for two minutes together." And Sir Joshua Reynolds wrote: "There is no expedient to which a man will not resort to avoid the real labor of thinking." Thomas A. Edison was so fond of this last quotation that he put up signs with it all over his plant.

Yes, thinking is hard work, and that's why the greatest enemy of thinking is sheer inertia. Some time ago, I ran across a story in the *New York Times* that dealt with a UN report on economic help to Bolivia.

The reasons for the lack of economic progress [the *Times* reported] lie mainly not in the lack of knowledge of what is needed, or even technical know-how in a restricted sense, but in the unwillingness or inability of governments to do what is needed. . . . The U.N. mission found that studies and recommendations on Bolivia's needs, going back forty years, were piled high in government archives. All studies recommended more or less the same thing, and little or nothing had ever been done about any of them. Knowledge of what to do was obviously not the problem.

In a sense, we are all in the same situation as the government of Bolivia. We know what to do about most of our problems, but we don't use that knowledge. We could improve our personal finances by budgeting, but we don't budget; we could improve our health by dieting, but we don't diet; we could improve our careers by studying, but we don't study. Information is piled high in our lives' archives, but we don't use it. Thinking is too hard.

Of course, we don't like to put it so bluntly. Instead, we rationalize. Thinking isn't too hard, we say, but it's impractical, unrealistic, longhair stuff, it won't work. The practical thing is to go ahead without thinking, leaving things the way they have always been, doing what everybody else has always done. Never mind the rational approach; the irrational way is familiar and so much nicer and easier.

Whenever scientists come up with new rational solutions to seemingly irrational problems, our first reaction is to resist their ideas. Our second reaction is to get rid of them as something thought up by cranks. We don't want anyone to encroach upon the province of the irrational; we like to have a large slice of life where we don't have to do any thinking. Nature, art, life and death, chance—let's simply accept them; the human mind shouldn't meddle with these things.

Meanwhile, in spite of all this hostility, scientists persist in the analytical and mathematical study of the irrational. We may shrug it off, but there is dynamic symmetry (the mathematical analysis of art design from the Parthenon to Le Corbusier's houses), there is the Schillinger system of musical composition on a mathematical basis, and there are statistical studies of patterns in people's conversations, of cycles in our emotional ups and downs, of the law that governs the degree of repetition in the programs of the Boston Symphony Orchestra, and of the relationship between the number of marriages and the number of city blocks between boys and girls in Philadelphia. There is the mathematical approach to the strategy of bluffing in poker, the study of mathematical biophysics, the factor analysis of human abilities and temperament, and Professor D'Arcy Thompson's classic book *On Growth and Form,* which deals with the mathematics of such things as splashes and bubbles, bee's cells, the shapes of eggs, blood corpuscles, chromosomes, falling drops, spirals, streamlines, corals, snow crystals, elephants' teeth and the horns of sheep and goats.

This is the sort of thing that makes us feel uneasy; although it's all fascinating, we'd much rather the mathematicians would leave these matters alone. When it comes to practical applications, we're apt to be stubborn and resentful. It is this distrust of the rational approach that accounts, in part, for our sales resistance to all forms of insurance and for our general resistance to such things as health insurance, business cycle theory, city planning, and proportional representation.

Of course, we all pride ourselves on having an open mind. But what do we mean by that? More often than not, an open mind means that we stick to our opinions and let other people have theirs. This fills us with a pleasant sense of tolerance and lack of bias—*but it isn't good enough.* What we need is not so much an open mind—readiness to accept new ideas—but an attitude of distrust toward *our own* ideas. This, as I said before, is the scientific habit of thought: as soon as you have an idea, try to disprove it. "To have doubted one's own first principles," Justice Oliver Wendell Holmes once wrote, "is the mark of a civilized man."

To do that is the hardest thing of all. Our first principles, our basic ideas, are those most intimately tied up with our personality, with the emotional make-up we have inherited or acquired. Detached, impersonal thinking is almost impossible; it hardly ever actually happens. In 1940 a team of social scientists studied the thinking of voters in Sandusky, Ohio, to find out why they voted the way they did. The scientists found that people voted according to their income, religion, age, occupation, and so on, following the pattern of their relatives, neighbors and friends. They did *not* vote on the basis of a detached, impartial weighing of the issues. "Dispassionate, rational voters," the survey concluded, "exist mainly in textbooks on civics, in the movies, and in the minds of some political idealists. In real life, they are few."

Yes, clear thinking is rare. To approach it, we need above all that indispensable quality of the scientific spirit—humility. Like good scientists, we must be ready to sacrifice some of our personality and habits of thought as we face each new problem. For life's problems are always new, and defy all ready-made solutions.

That's what makes life so interesting.

A P P E N D I X

READING LIST

Here is a short list of books for laymen that you may want to read after this one. There are two on thinking in general and a few more on certain specific topics.

Thinking in general:

An excellent book by a psychologist is:
Directed Thinking, by George Humphrey (New York: Dodd, Mead, & Company, Inc., 1948).
The most fascinating book on thinking is:
The Practical Cogitator, or The Thinker's Anthology, selected and edited by Charles P. Curtis, Jr. and Ferris Greenslet (Boston: Houghton Mifflin Company, 1945). Not easy to read, but filled to the brim with stimulating stuff.

Thinking machines:

In so far as they can be explained to laymen, they are explained in:
Giant Brains, or Machines That Think, by Edmund Callis Berkeley (New York: John Wiley & Sons, Inc., 1949).

Animal intelligence:

Many experiments are covered in a breezy collection of magazine articles:
Animal IQ: The Human Side of Animals, by Vance Packard (New York: Dial Press, Inc., 1950; also New York: Pocket Books, 1951).

The mind and the brain:

The best book for laymen is a series of brief B.B.C. radio talks:
The Physical Basis of Mind; a Symposium, edited by Peter Laslett (New York: The Macmillan Company, 1950).

Language:

A good book on scientific linguistics for laymen is:
Leave Your Language Alone! by Robert A. Hall, Jr. (Ithaca, N. Y.: Linguistica, 1950).
There is also a highly interesting anthology on linguistics and semantics:

The Language of Wisdom and Folly; Background Readings in Semantics, edited by Irving J. Lee (New York: Harper & Brothers, 1949).

Logic:

The best book on logic for laymen is:
How to Think Straight; The Technique of Applying Logic Instead of Emotion, by Robert H. Thouless (New York: Simon & Schuster, Inc., 1945; originally published in 1932 under the title *Straight and Crooked Thinking*).

Law:

Legal reasoning is taken to pieces in:
Woe Unto You, Lawyers! by Fred Rodell (New York: Reynal & Hitchcock, 1939). One of the most amusing books on thinking ever written.

Productive thinking and problem-solving:

The first general book on this subject is still useful today:
The Art of Thought, by Graham Wallas (New York: Harcourt, Brace & Company, Inc., 1926; abridged edition in The Thinker's Library [London: Watts & Company, 1949]).
A very practical and readable book was written by an advertising man:
Your Creative Power; How to Use Imagination, by Alex Osborn (New York: Charles Scribner's Sons, 1948).

Scientific method:

The president of Harvard University recently explained that there *is* no scientific method and why:
Science and Common Sense, by James B. Conant (New Haven: Yale University Press, 1951).

Statistics:

If you can't stand *any* mathematics, there isn't any book for you. If you can stand an absolute minimum, there is:
The Science of Chance; From Probability to Statistics, by Horace C. Levinson, Ph.D. (New York: Rinehart & Co., Inc., 1950).

MEASURING THE LEVEL OF ABSTRACTION

BY RUDOLF FLESCH

(Abridged from *Journal of Applied Psychology*, Vol. 34, No. 6, December, 1950, pp. 384-90)

Students of communication agree that awareness of the level of abstraction is essential for full comprehension. For example, Perrin, in his college text, says: "For exact and reasonable communication it is highly important that a speaker or writer knows where in the range of meaning of abstract words his core of meaning falls and that he makes this clear to his listeners or readers." Semanticists are especially emphatic on this point. Johnson writes: "The prime objective of general semantics is to make one conscious of abstracting." Hayakawa writes: "Consciousness of abstracting is . . . a sign of adulthood."

Though the significance of the level of abstraction is widely recognized, no studies have been reported that attempt to estimate or measure it quantitatively. Discussions are usually limited to generalized distinctions between abstract and concrete words, illustrative examples, and such figurative devices as the semanticists' "abstraction ladder."

The present study is an attempt to approach this problem with the technique developed for the measurement of readability. . . .

To test the level of abstraction, the writer analyzed the generally accepted grammatical categories of the parts of speech. It was found that most parts of speech contained certain categories that were statistically related to abstractness and certain others related to concreteness. In general, words related to abstractness are more indefinite, those related to concreteness more definite. The writer, therefore, chose the arbitrary label "definite words" for the words whose percentage was used to measure concreteness (level of abstraction).

The percentage of "definite words" may be considered useful to form a rough estimate of the level of abstraction, ranging from 0 (fully abstract) to 100 (fully concrete). . . .

An amusing illustration of the new measure is furnished by Hayakawa, who explains his "abstraction ladder" by way of four statements on different levels of abstraction. Application of the new measure to these examples shows the following:

	Ratio of "definite words"	Percentage of "definite words"
Mrs. *Plotz makes* good potato pancakes.	3 in 6	50
Mrs. *Plotz* is a good cook.	2 in 6	33
Chicago women are good cooks.	1 in 5	20
The culinary art *has* reached a high state in America.	1 in 10	10

How to Use the Formula

For practical application, the directions for using the formula may be stated as follows:

To measure the level of abstraction of a given piece of writing, go through the following steps:

Step 1. Unless you want to test a whole piece of writing, take samples. Take enough samples to make a fair test. Don't try to pick "good" or "typical" samples. Go by a strictly numerical scheme. For instance, take every third paragraph or every other page. Each sample should start at the beginning of a paragraph.

Step 2. Count the words in your piece of writing or, if you are using samples, take each sample and count each word in it up to 100. Count contractions and hyphenated words as one word. Count as words numbers or letters separated by space.

Step 3. Count the following "definite words." Count each of these words only once. Count as words all units separated by white space. (In the examples, "definite words" are italicized.)

(1) Count all names of people—that is, proper nouns with natural gender, either masculine or feminine. Count all words that are part of the name, including titles, etc., used as part of the name. Example: *President Harry S. Truman* (count 4).

Count names of people used as adjectives to modify natural-gender nouns (e.g., the *Smith brothers,* the *Dolly sisters*), but do not count personal names used as adjectives to modify nouns *without* natural gender (e.g., the Ford Motor Company, the Washington Monument).

(2) Count all common nouns that have natural gender, either masculine or feminine. Examples: *father, mother, iceman, actress.* Count these words also when used as adjectives to indicate the gender of another noun (e.g., *woman doctor, bull elephant, girl athlete*), but do not count them when they do not indicate gender (e.g., fellow workers).

Do not count common-gender nouns like teacher, doctor, employee, spouse.

(3) Count all nouns that indicate a specific time on the clock or the calendar; e.g., the names of the months, the seasons, the days of the week, the words *morning, noon, afternoon, evening, night, day* (in the sense of daytime), *sunup, sundown, today, tonight, yesterday, tomorrow,* and the words *breakfast, lunch, dinner, supper* when used to indicate time. Count these words also when used as adjectives to specify time (e.g., *December day, fall season, lunch hour*), but do not count them when used as adjectives without relation to time (e.g., Thursday club, dinner companion, Sunday suit).

(4) Count all numeral adjectives and all nouns modified by numeral adjectives. Count also the words *first, next, last,* and such words as *double, pair, half, triple.* Examples: 27 *words.* 54 *per cent. Six letters.* The *next day.* The *last moment.* But don't count nouns that are not directly modified by numerals, e.g., *thousands* of people, a *ten-year-old* house.

Count the word *one* in the sense of "single," but not when used as an indefinite pronoun or as part of "no one," "any one," or "some one." Examples: Count *one* in "*one* fine morning" and in "the pretty *one,*" but not in "one has one's doubts."

Count the word *once* in the sense of "a single time," but not in the phrase "at once." Examples: *Once* upon a time. *He succeeded once.*

Count the words *other* and *another* only in the sense of "second" or "one more."

(5) Count all finite verb forms—that is, verbs in the first, second, or third person and the present, past, or future tense. In verb forms with auxiliary verbs, count the auxiliary rather than the main verb. Examples: *He came* and *went. We have* considered. *You should* have declined. *Let us* pack up and go. *It was* debated and voted down.

Exception: Do not count the verb "to be" when used as copula, that is, as a link between subject and predicate. Do not count "to be" as copula in any form, with or without an auxiliary verb. Examples: *I was* sick. *You* should have been *there. It* might be fun. *He* ought to have been careful.

(6) Count all present participles (-*ing*) when used as part of the progressive tense (to be -*ing*). Examples: *He was running. I am going* to look. *You should* have been *working.*

(7) Count all personal pronouns except indefinite "it," and all re-

flexive pronouns, formed with -*self* or -*selves*. Examples: It is a fact that *you* and *I* are not related. It was *Mary herself*.

(8) Count the words *here, there, then,* and *now* (except indefinite "there" in "there is," "there are," etc.).

(9) Count the words *who, whom, when, where, why,* and *how*.

(10) Count the words *this, that, these,* and *those; each, same,* and *both;* and nouns modified by them.

(11) Count the words *what* and *which* (interrogative) and nouns modified by them, but not the word "which" when used as a relative pronoun. Examples: *Which way are you going?* But: The car which *I bought*.

(12) Count all possessive pronouns (*my, your, his, her, its, our, their,* etc.), all nouns in the possessive case ending in 's or s', the word *whose,* and all nouns modified by these possessives. Examples: *Our* modern *civilization, its* recent *development, whose business, journey's end*.

But do not count possessive cases of pronouns not otherwise counted, e.g., "one's ideas," "someone else's hat."

(13) Count the word *that* when used as a relative pronoun, but not when used as a conjunction. Examples: Remember that *you* are sick. It was the humidity *that did* it.

(14) Count the words *yes* and *no* (used as answer).

(15) Count all interjections.

(16) Count the definite article *the* and the noun modified by it, but only if that noun is a single word not otherwise modified. Examples: *I missed the bus. We called the doctor. It* was *the truth*. But: *I missed* the green bus. *We called* the eye specialist. *It* was the truth, plain and simple. *They gave me* the room *I had last time. It* was the beginning of *the end. We live* at the end of *the village,* in the yellow house at the turn of *the road*.

Do not count the word "the" when modifying a noun that is to be counted under one of the other definitions. Examples: *He came* in the *afternoon. The only one there* was the *boy*.

Do not count the word "the" when modifying adjectives or noun-adjectives, particularly proper noun-adjectives referring to nationality, race, etc. Examples: *Their team* was the best. *We sat* in the dark. *What's* the good of *it? The Scotch* are thrifty. *The Negro was* arrested.

Step 4. The number of "definite words" in your 100-word sample (or the average percentage of "definite words" in all your samples or the whole piece of writing tested) indicates the level of abstraction. The typical relation between the percentage of "definite words" and level of abstraction is shown below.

Typical Percentages of "Definite Words"

Level of Abstraction	Percentage of "Definite Words"
Highly abstract	Up to 20
Fairly abstract	20 to 30
Fairly concrete	30 to 45
Highly concrete	Over 45

Sample Application

To show the application of the new test, three passages dealing with the subject of truth will be used. Passage A, exemplifying a highly concrete style, is Test Lesson No. 37 from Book III of the *Standard Test Lessons in Reading* that were used as criterion. Passage B was taken from *Courts on Trial* by Jerome Frank. It is an example of writing on the middle level of abstraction, illustrating the more abstract generalizations in the first paragraph by more concrete examples in the second. Passage C was taken from *The Next Development in Man* by L. L. Whyte and shows a highly abstract, philosophical discussion of truth.

"Definite words" in the three passages are italicized.

Passage A:

The children were telling about *their Christmas vacations.*
"We went to Kansas," *said Jack. "One day when were skating* on *the lake* some of the *boys cut* a hole in *the ice, struck* a match and a fire *blazed* right up out of *the hole* for *two* or *three minutes."*
"Oh, oh!" said all the others, *"that* couldn't be true. Water *doesn't* burn."
"But it is true," *said Jack. "I saw it."*
They turned to *the teacher* to see *what she would* say and *she explained this* very strange *happening. It seems* there are natural gas wells under *the lake* which *send the gas* bubbling up through *the water where it is* caught in large pockets under *the ice.*
"So you see," said the teacher, "when a hole *is* cut the escaping gas *will* burn if lighted."

Passage B:

No means *then, have* as yet been discovered, or are likely to be discovered, for ascertaining whether or to *what extent* the belief of the trial judge about the facts of a case *corresponds* to the objective facts as *they* actually *occurred, when the witnesses disagree,* and *when* some of the oral testimony, taken as true, *will* support the *judge's conclusion.* In other words, in such a case there is no objective measure of the accuracy of a *judge's finding* of *the facts*. There *exists* no yardstick for *that purpose*.

In a "contested" law suit, therefore, with *the witnesses* in disagreement, usually no one *can* adequately criticize the trial *judge's fact-finding*. If, at the end of *the trial*, the trial judge *says* that *Jones hit Smith*, or that *Mrs. Moriarity called Mrs. Flannagan* a liar, or that old *widow Robinson* was insane *when she made her will*, or that *Wriggle used* fraud in inducing *Simple* to sign a contract—the *judge's word goes*. And the *same* would be true if, in most of *those instances*, the trial judge *had* found exactly the opposite to be *the facts*.

Passage C:

Truth is thought which *conforms* to the form of the whole. Conformity to the whole is *the criterion*. The unitary truth is *that* which *conforms* to the whole process of which *it* is a part. *The truth* is a form embedded in the whole complex of processes in the human organism and *its environment*, symbolizing and organizing *them*. A particular truth *may* not represent the entire structure of a situation but only *those aspects* which are relevant to thought at a given stage in *its development. The truth* is a system of symbols *whose structure conforms* to the whole pattern of feeling, thought, and action, and *integrates* all the processes which *link* the reception of stimuli and the molding of the ultimate responses. *This* is not a pragmatic criterion, since unitary truth *does* not merely serve special needs but *unites* the whole system in a conviction which is at once emotional, intellectual, and practical.

A comparative analysis of the three passages is given below.

Analysis of Three Sample Passages

	Percentage of "Definite Words"
Passage A	53 (highly concrete)
Passage B:	
First paragraph	24 (fairly abstract)
Second paragraph	37 (fairly concrete)
Both paragraphs	31 (fairly concrete)
Passage C	17 (highly abstract)

Considerable experience with practical application of the new test has shown that an untrained person can acquire reasonable familiarity with this test after ten to twenty applications and will then be able to count the "definite words" in a 100-word sample in one to two minutes.

NOTES

CHAPTER 1: ROBOTS, APES AND YOU

Page

1   *Ticktacktoe machine.* New York *World-Telegram*, December 13, 1949, p. 10; *Newsweek*, August 29, 1949, p. 51.

2   *Mathematical machines.* See *Cybernetics* by Norbert Wiener (New York: John Wiley & Sons, Inc., 1948); *Giant Brains* by Edmund C. Berkeley (New York: John Wiley & Sons, Inc., 1949). Also many newspaper and magazine stories.

3   *Automatic chess player.* "A chess-playing machine" by Claude E. Shannon, *Scientific American*, February, 1950, pp. 48-51.

4   *"Simple Simon."* "Simple Simon" by Edmund C. Berkeley, *Scientific American*, November, 1950, Vol. 183, pp. 40 ff.

5   *Köhler's study of apes.* The *Mentality of Apes* by Wolfgang Köhler (New York: Harcourt, Brace & Company, Inc., 1927). For later criticism, see, for instance, "Learning to think" by Harry F. and Margaret Kuenne Harlow, *Scientific American*, August, 1949, Vol. 181, pp. 36-39.

6   *Birch's experiments.* "The relation of previous experience to insightful problem-solving" by Herbert G. Birch, *Journal of Comparative Psychology*, December, 1945, Vol. 38, No. 6, pp. 367-83.

7   *Bronowski.* See "The mature machine," *Time*, January 12, 1951, p. 65. See also "A machine that learns" by W. Grey Walter, *Scientific American*, August, 1951, pp. 60 ff.

CHAPTER 2: NERVES AND THOUGHTS

9   *B.B.C. symposium.* See *The Physical Basis of Mind; a Symposium* edited by Peter Laslett (New York: The Macmillan Company, 1950).

10   *Penfield's studies.* These are summarized in *The Cerebral Cortex of Man; a Clinical Study of Localization of Function* by Wilder Penfield and Theodore Rasmussen (New York: The Macmillan Company, 1950).

11   *Kappa waves.* "A new electroencephalogram associated with thinking" by John L. Kennedy, Robert M. Gottsdanker, John C. Armington,

and Florence E. Gray, *Science*, November 12, 1948, Vol. 108, pp. 527-29; also *Newsweek*, November 7, 1949, p. 56.

13 *Lobotomy*. The quotations are from "Psychosurgery" by Walter Freeman and James W. Watts, *Progress in Neurology and Psychiatry* (New York: Grune & Stratton, Inc., 1948), pp. 409-20; "Psychosurgery. A. Neuropsychiatric Aspects" by Walter Freeman, *Progress in Neurology and Psychiatry* (New York: Grune & Stratton, Inc., 1949), pp. 389-95; "Prefrontal lobotomy: Analysis and warning" by Kurt Goldstein, *Scientific American*, February, 1950, pp. 48-51; "The great ravelled knot" by George W. Gray, *Scientific American*, October, 1948, Vol. 179, pp. 26-39; and the Penfield-Rasmussen book, mentioned above.

14 *Reverberation theory*. See, for instance, "The coalescence of neurology and psychology" by Karl S. Lashley *Proceedings of the American Philosophical Society*, 1941, Vol. 84, pp. 461-70; also *The Organization of Behavior; a Neurophysiological Theory* by D. O. Hebb (New York: John Wiley & Sons, Inc., 1949).

CHAPTER 3: Do You See What I See?

16 *Galton. Inquiries into Human Faculty* by Sir Francis Galton (London, New York: The Macmillan Company, 1883; also in Everyman's Library, 1908).

19 *Blackman*. "The shape of a year" by M. C. Blackman, *The New Yorker*, June 26, 1948, p. 48.

20 *Salo Finkelstein*. "The memory of Salo Finkelstein" by James D. Weinland, *Journal of General Psychology*, 1948, Vol. 39, pp. 243-57; "The visual imagery of a lightning calculator" by W. A. Bousfield and H. Barry, *American Journal of Psychology*, 1933, Vol. 45, pp. 353-58.

21 *Bartlett. Remembering* by F. C. Bartlett (Cambridge, England: Cambridge University Press, 1932), p. 213.
   Proust. Letters of Marcel Proust edited by Mina Curtiss (New York: Random House, 1949), p. 226-27.
   Adelbert Ames' experiments. See, for instance, *Education for What Is Real* by Earl C. Kelley (New York: Harper & Brothers, 1947).

22 *Picture from "Life."* It appeared on January 10, 1949, p. 104.
   Picture distortion experiment. "An experimental study of the effect of language on the reproduction of visually perceived form" by Leonard Carmichael, H. P. Hogan, and A. A. Walter, *Journal of Experimental Psychology*, 1932, Vol. 15, pp. 73-86.

22   *Rumor experiment. The Psychology of Rumor* by Gordon W. Allport and Leo Postman (New York: Henry Holt & Company, Inc., 1947).

    Money experiment. "Value and need as organizing factors in perception" by Jerome S. Bruner and Cecile S. Goodman, *Journal of Abnormal and Social Psychology,* 1947, Vol. 42, pp. 33-44.

25   *Stories from same plot. Fourteen Stories from One Plot; Based on "Mr. Fothergill's Plot"* edited by John M. Berdan (New York: Oxford University Press, 1932).

CHAPTER 4: OF THINGUMMIES AND WHATCHAMACALLITS

27   *"A polyp . . ." Psychology; Briefer Course* by William James (New York: Henry Holt & Company, Inc., 1904), p. 240.

28   *Pran.* "The attainment of concepts: I. Terminology and methodology" by Edna Heidbreder, *Journal of General Psychology,* 1946, Vol. 35, pp. 173-89.

31   *Chair. Mechanization Takes Command* by Siegfried Giedion (New York: Oxford University Press, 1948).

    Opera. Oxford History of Music, Vol. 3 (New York: Oxford University Press, 1902).

    Novel. History of Prose Fiction by John Colin Dunlop (London: George Bell & Sons, Ltd., 1911).

    Zero. History of Mathematics by Florian Cajori (New York: The Macmillan Company, 1906).

32   *Corporations. Some Origins of the Modern Economic World* by E. J. Johnson (New York: The Macmillan Company, 1936).

    Love. Love in the Western World by Denis de Rougemont (New York: Harcourt, Brace & Company, Inc., 1940). See also "Romantic Love" by Hugo G. Beigel, *American Sociological Review,* Vol. 16, No. 3, June 1951, pp. 326-34.

33   *Progress. The Idea of Progress; an Inquiry into its Origin and Growth* by John Bagnell Bury (New York: The Macmillan Company, 1920).

    Success. See *Religion and the Rise of Capitalism; a Historical Study* by R. H. Tawney (New York: Harcourt, Brace & Company, Inc., 1926), Chapter IV; also *Protestant Ethic and the Spirit of Capitalism* by Max Weber (Charles Scribner's Sons, 1930). *The Tradesman's Calling* by Richard Steele was published in London in 1684 and often reprinted.

Page

46   *Cowper on Pope's Homer translation*. See *Early Theories of Translation* by Flora Ross Amos (New York: Columbia University Press, 1920), p. 176.

      Highet on Lawrence's Homer. Review of *The Wrath of Achilles* by I. A. Richards, *New York Times Book Review*, November 19, 1950.

47   *Macbeth in German*. The eight translations referred to are by Schlegel-Tieck, Schiller, Kaufmann, W. Jordan, H. Voss, G. Messmer, Hans Rothe and Friedrich Gundolf.

48   *Broadway adaptation of "The Madwoman of Chaillot."* New York *Herald Tribune*, August 21, 1949.

      Viennese adaptation of "Death of a Salesman." New York *Herald Tribune*, March 19, 1950.

CHAPTER 7: FIRST AID FOR WORD TROUBLE

58   *Questions. Thinking as a Science* by Henry Hazlitt (New York. E. P. Dutton & Co., Inc., 1916); *The Logic of Modern Physics* by Percy W. Bridgman (New York: The Macmillan Company, 1927); see also *People in Quandaries* by Wendell Johnson (New York, Harper & Brothers, 1946), p. 289.

CHAPTER 8: THE RISE AND FALL OF FORMAL LOGIC

59   *Plato's "Meno."* This is the Jowett translation.

61   *Greek debate game. Logic, Inductive and Deductive* by William Minto (New York: Charles Scribner's Sons, 1893), p. 3; *Greek Foundations of Traditional Logic* by Ernst Kapp (New York: Columbia University Press, 1942).

62   *Tests of logical reasoning. How to Think Straight* by Robert H. Thouless (New York: Simon & Schuster, Inc., 1939).

63   *Locke*. The quotation is from *An Essay Concerning Human Understanding*, Bk. 4, Ch. 17, Sect. 4.

      Bacon. The quotation is from *Novum Organum*, Bk. I, XII.

      Max Wertheimer. Productive Thinking (New York: Harper & Brothers, 1946), p. 10.

      George Humphrey. Directed Thinking (New York: Dodd, Mead & Company, Inc., 1948), p. 88.

64   *Symbolic logic*. See, among many other sources, *Introduction to Symbolic Logic* by Susanne K. Langer (Boston: Houghton Mifflin Company, 1937). The quotation is from p. 345.

Page

65 *Examination problem.* "Boolean algebra (the technique for manipu-
    lating 'and,' 'or,' 'not' and conditions) and applications to insur-
    ance" by Edmund C. Berkeley, *The Record*, American Institute of
    Actuaries, October, 1937, Vol. 26, Pt. 2, pp. 373-414.
    Use of symbolic logic for computing machines. "The relations between
    symbolic logic and large-scale calculating machines" by Edmund C.
    Berkeley, *Science*, October 6, 1950, pp. 395-99.

CHAPTER 9: HOW NOT TO BE BAMBOOZLED

66 *Cohen and Nagel's text. An Introduction to Logic and Scientific
    Method* by Morris R. Cohen and Ernest Nagel (New York: Har-
    court, Brace & Company, Inc., 1934).

69 *Prestige ads.* I am partly indebted here to "Minutes of the Annual
    Meeting of the Endorsers' Club, held at the Clubhouse on February
    2, 1949" by Corey Ford, *The New Yorker*, February 12, 1949,
    p. 44.

70 *Television ad.* It appeared on November 13, 1950.

72 *Article on child labor.* "The Federal snoops are after me" by Robinson
    McIlvaine, *Saturday Evening Post*, March 18, 1950; also *Reader's
    Digest*, October, 1950. For data on the case see *The Nation*, April
    8, 1950, and Memorandum to the Secretary of Labor by Mr.
    William R. McComb, Administrator, dated March 16, 1950.

73 *Quotation from George Orwell.* "Nonsense poetry," in: *Shooting an
    Elephant and Other Essays* (New York: Harcourt, Brace & Com-
    pany, Inc., 1950), p. 191.

CHAPTER 10: WHY ARGUE?

74 *Justification of teaching logic.* See, for instance, "The effects of a
    course in argumentation on critical thinking ability" by Winston L.
    Brembeck, *Speech Monographs Research Annual*, 1949, Vol. 16,
    No. 2, pp. 177-89, and "Functional logic" by John Henry Melzer,
    Journal of Higher Education, March, 1949, Vol. 20, pp. 143-47.

75 *Perkins on Shakespeare. Editor to Author; the Letters of Maxwell E.
    Perkins*, selected and edited by John Hall Wheelock (New York:
    Charles Scribner's Sons, 1950), p. 204.

76 *Sidewalk interview.* New York Post, September 18, 1950.

77 *Debate on New York Post.* "Can newspapers survive without sex?" *Saturday Review of Literature,* June 24, 1950.

78 *Debate on housing.* "The Sky Line," *The New Yorker,* June 24, 1950, pp. 78 ff.

79 *Debate on differences in intelligence.* "Does genetic endowment vary by socioeconomic group?" *Science,* June 23, 1950, Vol. 111, pp. 697-99.

80 *Outline of History. The Outline of History* by H. G. Wells, revised and brought up to the end of the Second World War by Raymond Postgate (Garden City: Garden City Publishing Company, Inc., 1949). See also footnotes in the original 1921 edition.

CHAPTER 11: LEGAL RULES AND LIVELY CASES

83 *Application of legal rules.* The first quotation is from *How Lawyers Think* by Clarence Morris (Cambridge, Massachusetts: Harvard University Press, 1938), p. 71; the others are from *An Introduction to Legal Reasoning* by Edward H. Levi (Chicago: University of Chicago Press, 1949). See also *Courts on Trial; Myth and Reality in American Justice* by Jerome Frank (Princeton: Princeton University Press, 1949) and *Woe Unto You, Lawyers!* by Fred Rodell (New York: Reynal & Hitchcock, 1939).

84 *Cases.* C. F. Mueller Co.: *New York Times,* May 28, 1950. Smith: New York *Herald Tribune,* September 3, 1950. Glagovsky: New York *Herald Tribune,* December 10, 1950. Petro: Associated Press, November 16, 1950.

85 *"Inherently dangerous" rule.* See Levi, cited above.

86 *Displaced Persons Act.* Personal letter from Department of State, January 12, 1950.
Minimum Wage Law. Senator Thomas was quoted in the *New York Times,* October 15, 1949. The quotations from the *Congressional Record* are from the House debate, August 8, 1949, pp. 11216-17.

88 *Magazine writer on jury.* "In the jury room" by Anna Mary Wells, *The New Yorker,* September 17, 1949.

89 *Juries and contributory negligence. A Judge Takes the Stand* by Joseph N. Ulman (New York: Alfred A. Knopf, Inc., 1933), p. 33.
Cozzens' novel. The Just and the Unjust by James Gould Cozzens (New York: Harcourt, Brace & Company, Inc., 1942), pp. 427-28.

CHAPTER 12: ENTER A BRIGHT IDEA

Page

90   *Senator Douglas' idea.* "A Senator's vote: a searching of the soul" by
      Senator Paul H. Douglas, *New York Times Magazine*, April 30,
      1950.

91   *Psychological studies of problem-solving.* A good survey is "A modern
      account of problem solving" by Donald M. Johnson, *Psychological
      Bulletin*, April, 1944, Vol. 41, pp. 201-29.

92   *Duncker's experiments.* "On problem-solving" by Karl Duncker, *Psy-
      chological Monographs*, 1945, Vol. 58, No. 5, Whole Number 270.

93   *Gottschaldt Figures Test.* See *A Factorial Study of Perception* by L. L.
      Thurstone (Chicago: University of Chicago Press, 1944).

99   *Wertheimer's illustration. Productive Thinking* by Max Wertheimer
      (New York: Harper & Brothers, 1946).

100   *Brain wave studies of geniuses. New York Times*, February 24, 1951,
      p. 9; also *Life*, February 26, 1951, p. 40.
      Roosevelt thinks up Lend-Lease. See especially *Roosevelt and Hopkins;
      an Intimate History* by Robert E. Sherwood (New York: Harper &
      Brothers, 1948), pp. 223-25.

CHAPTER 13: HOW TO SOLVE A PUZZLE

102   *Teralbay.* This is from the essay "A lost masterpiece" in *If I May* by
      A. A. Milne (New York: E. P. Dutton & Co., Inc., 1921). The
      solution is: *betrayal.*

104   *"More people live in London . . . etc." Psychology of Reasoning* by
      Eugenio Rignano (New York: Harcourt, Brace & Company, Inc.,
      1923), p. 72.
      Husband's and wife's ages. They are 56 and 42.

105   *Smallest number, etc.* 301.
      How did Robinson fare? He lost $8.

106   *Poe as detective.* See, for instance, *The Scholar Adventurers* by
      Richard D. Altick (New York: The Macmillan Company, 1950).
      Doyle as detective. See *The Life of Sir Arthur Conan Doyle* by John
      Dickson Carr (New York: Harper & Brothers, 1949), pp. 178 ff.

107   *Van Gogh picture.* New York *Herald Tribune*, December 1, 1949,
      and October 4, 1950.

109   *Mystery story formula.* The quotation is from "The craft of crime" by
      Richard Lockridge, in: *The Writer's Book* edited by Helen Hull
      (New York: Harper & Brothers, 1950), p. 60.

Page

111   *"Educing of correlates." Creative Mind* by C. Spearman (New York: D. Appleton-Century Co., Inc., 1931).
Hobbes. Quoted in Wallas' *Art of Thought* (see Reading List).

112   *Bancroft.* "The methods of research" by Wilder D. Bancroft, *Rice Institute Pamphlet*, October, 1928, Vol. 15, No. 4, p. 290.
Twenty questions. The quoted excerpts are from the program of October 7, 1950.

117   *Accident rate. Mind and Body: Psychosomatic Medicine* by Flanders Dunbar (New York: Random House, Inc., 1948), pp. 99-100.

118   *Osborn's book. Your Creative Power* by Alex Osborn (see Reading List).

119   *Weather in novels. Aspects of the Novel* by E. M. Forster (New York: Harcourt, Brace & Company, Inc., 1927).

120   *Classification of love. The Family and Democratic Society* by Joseph K. Folsom (New York: John Wiley & Sons, Inc., 1934).

122   *Teeple takes two baths.* The incident is described in "The relation of scientific 'hunch' to research" by Washington Platt and Ross A. Baker, *Journal of Chemical Education*, October, 1931, Vol. 8, No. 10, pp. 1969-2002.

124   *Principle of complementarity.* "On the notions of causality and complementarity" by Niels Bohr, *Science*, January 20, 1950, Vol. 111, pp. 51-54.

125   *What is scientific method? Science and Common Sense* by James B. Conant (New Haven: Yale University Press, 1951). *The Art of Scientific Investigation* by W. I. B. Beveridge (New York: W. W. Norton & Company, Inc., 1950). See also *The Genius of Industrial Research* by D. H. Killeffer (New York: Reinhold Publishing Corporation, 1948).
"Whittling away at cancer." Time, February 12, 1951, p. 59.
Dr. Sinnott on lack of new ideas in U.S. science. New York Times, September 30, 1950.

126   *Accidents.* The data are to be found in any history of science.
Fleming: "My, that's a funny thing." New York Post, "The Lyons Den," February 19, 1951.

127   *Hunches. Harvey: An Anatomical Disquisition on the Motion of the Heart and Blood in Animals*, translated by Robert Willis (London,

Page

1847). Watt: *History of Mechanical Inventions* by Abbot P. Usher (New York: McGraw-Hill Book Company, 1929). Darwin: *The Art of Scientific Investigation* by W. I. B. Beveridge (New York: W. W. Norton & Company, Inc., 1950), p. 68. Kekulé: *The Path of Science* by C. E. Kenneth Mees (New York: John Wiley & Sons, Inc., 1946), p. 125. Cannon: *The Way of an Investigator* by Walter B. Cannon (New York: W. W. Norton & Company, Inc., 1945), pp. 59-60.

128　*Propaganda study.* "Experiments on Mass Communication," *Studies in Social Psychology in World War II*, Vol. III by Carl I. Hovland, Arthur A. Lumsdaine, and Fred D. Sheffield (Princeton: Princeton University Press, 1949), pp. 273-75.

CHAPTER 16: THE HARNESSING OF CHANCE

129　*"Life" picture of albino deer.* It appeared on April 24, 1950.
　　　Leonard Bacon. "The long arm of coincidence" by Leonard Bacon, *Saturday Review of Literature*, December 14, 1946, pp. 9-10.

130　*Case of Rev. Ernest Lyons.* See *Convicting the Innocent* by Edwin M. Borchard (New Haven: Yale University Press, 1932), pp. 148 ff.
　　　Thirty-two times red in Monte Carlo. "Probability" by Warren Weaver, *Scientific American*, October, 1950, pp. 44-47.

131　*Normal curve.* "Chance, coincidence and normal curve" by Roland L. Beck, *School & Society*, November 6, 1948, Vol. 48, No. 1767, pp. 323-26.
　　　Errors in census. New York Times, July 22, 1950, p. 17.
　　　One-million error of unemployment statistics. Time, October 3, 1949, p. 67, and personal letter from Bureau of Labor Statistics, November 16, 1949.

132　*Three-fourths will call heads, etc.* "The human element in probability" by Louis D. Goodfellow, *Journal of General Psychology*, 1940, Vol. 23, pp. 201-5.
　　　Sample of names by alphabet biased. Surveys, Polls and Samples: Practical Procedures by Mildred Parten (New York: Harper & Brothers, 1950), p. 223.
　　　Quota sampling and area sampling. See, for instance, "Dependable samples for market surveys" by Morris H. Hansen and William N. Hurwitz, *Journal of Marketing*, October, 1949, pp. 362-72.
　　　Fifteen per cent more well-educated, etc. "Do interviewers bias poll results?" by Daniel Katz, *Public Opinion Quarterly*, 1942, Vol. 6, pp. 248-68.

133　*Mill's rules.* The quotation is from his *System of Logic*, Bk. III, Ch. VIII, Sect. 7. John Dewey's footnote: *How We Think* (Boston:

Page

D. C. Heath & Company, 1910), p. 90. Professor Chandler is quoted from Platt and Baker, mentioned above.

134 *Women of Polykastron.* New York *Herald Tribune,* May 15, 1950, p. 1.
Insulin and shock. New York *Times,* October 1, 1950, p. 92.
Storks and babies in Stockholm. "Intrinsic validity" by Harold Gulliksen, *American Psychologist,* October, 1950, Vol. 5, pp. 511-17.
Machinists' union and death rate in Hyderabad. A *Preface to Logic* by Morris R. Cohen (New York: Henry Holt & Company, Inc., 1944), p. 133.

135 *Correlations of intelligence test scores and state characteristics.* "Factors in state characteristics related to average A-12 V-12 test scores" by K. S. Davenport and H. H. Remmers, *Journal of Educational Psychology,* February, 1950, pp. 110-15.

136 *Glueck study of juvenile delinquency. Unraveling Juvenile Delinquency* by Sheldon Glueck and Eleanor Touroff Glueck (New York: Commonwealth Fund, 1950).

CHAPTER 17: HOW NOT TO RACK YOUR BRAIN

139 *Creative thinking.* John Livingston Lowes' study of Coleridge: *The Road to Xanadu* (Boston: Houghton Mifflin Company, 1927). "Mathematical creation" by Henri Poincaré appears in his *The Foundations of Science* (New York: Science Press, 1913). See also especially *An Essay on the Psychology of Invention in the Mathematical Field* by Jacques Hadamard (Princeton: Princeton University Press, 1945).
Stages of thought. The Art of Thought by Wallas (see Reading List). *A Technique for Producing Ideas* by James Webb Young (Chicago: Advertising Publications, 1940). "Developing creative engineers" by J. F. Young, *Mechanical Engineer,* December, 1945, pp. 305-14. *How to Think Creatively* by Eliot Dole Hutchinson (New York: Abingdon-Cokesbury Press, 1949).

140 *Presidential address.* The quotation is from "Creativity" by J. P. Guilford, *American Psychologist,* September, 1950, Vol. 5, pp. 444-54.

141 *Haldane's discoveries by writing simply. What Is Life?* by J. B. S. Haldane (New York: Boni & Gaer, 1947).
Bean used graphs. "Talk with Louis Bean" by Harvey Breit, *New York Times Book Review,* October 1, 1950, p. 31.
Silly things we remember. Mathematician's Delight by W. W. Sawyer (Harmondsworth, England: Penguin Books, 1943), p. 50.

Page

142 *Poincaré couldn't add.* See his *Mathematical Creation,* mentioned
       above.
     Maugham doesn't know the alphabet. A Writer's Notebook by W.
       Somerset Maugham (Garden City: Doubleday & Company, Inc.,
       1949), p. 330.
     Alekhine forgot his cigarettes. "Psychologie des grands joueurs
       d'échecs" by Xavier Tartacover, *Psyché,* 1949, Vol. 4, pp. 719-39.
     Miss Becker finds a book. New York Herald Tribune Book Review,
       December 3, 1950.

143 *Will Cuppy's card file.* The Decline and Fall of Practically Everybody
       by Will Cuppy (New York: Henry Holt & Company, Inc., 1950).
       See introduction by Fred Feldkamp.
     Discussion methods. See, for instance, *Creative Power Through Dis-
       cussion* by Thomas Fansler (New York: Harper & Brothers, 1950).
     How many people in the group? See "A preliminary study of the size
       determinant in small group interaction" by John James, *American
       Sociological Review,* August, 1951, Vol. 16, pp. 474-77.

145 *Fat folder in H drawer.* The New Yorker, August 19, 1950, p. 18.
     Strike a child in anger. Shaw's statement is from his *Maxims for
       Revolutionists* in the appendix to *Man and Superman.*
     Quotation from Whitehead. Adventures of Ideas (New York: The
       Macmillan Company, 1933).
     Relation between creative thought and humor. See *Insight and Out-
       look* by Arthur Koestler (New York: The Macmillan Company,
       1949).

146 *Survey of chemists.* See Platt and Baker's paper, mentioned above.
     Helmholtz. See Wallas' *Art of Thought* (in Reading List).

147 *Writers' schedules.* For Hemingway, Toynbee, and Bowers, see New
       York Herald Tribune Book Review, October 8, 1950; for O'Hara,
       MacInnes, and Brush, see *Writers and Writing* by Robert Van
       Gelder (New York: Charles Scribner's Sons, 1946).

          CHAPTER 18: THE THREE R'S—A REFRESHER COURSE

150 *Bloomfield on reading instruction.* Language by Leonard Bloomfield
       (New York: Henry Holt & Company, Inc., 1933), p. 499, and
       "About foreign language teaching" by Leonard Bloomfield, *Yale
       Review,* Summer, 1945, Vol. 34, No. 4, pp. 625-41. See also
       obituary article by Bernard Bloch, *Language,* April-June, 1949.
     Speeder-uppers and slower-downers. How to Read Better and Faster
       by Norman Lewis (New York: Thomas Y. Crowell Company,
       1944) and *How to Read a Book* by Mortimer J. Adler (New York:
       Simon & Schuster, Inc., 1940).

Page

150 *Eye movements.* "The study of eye movements in reading" by Miles A. Tinker, *Psychological Bulletin,* March, 1946, Vol. 43, pp. 93-120.

153 *Nicolson's advice.* The school was the Brooks School, North Andover, Mass. *New York Times Magazine,* May 14, 1950.

154 *Notehand systems.* For example, "Notehand for psychologists" by W. S. Taylor, *American Psychologist,* 1947, Vol. 2, pp. 106-7.

156 *Census figures on small-town population.* See census releases, Series PC-3, Nos. 3, 9, and 10, November, 1950 and February, 1951.
   Twins. "How bachelors get that way" by E. Ardis Whitman, *Coronet,* December, 1949, p. 44.
   Averages. I found these figures in *What Are the Odds?* by Leo Guild (New York: Pocket Books, 1949).
   Lawyers' income. New York Times, August 24, 1949.

157 *Popularly, the average means the mode. Thinking to Some Purpose* by L. Susan Stebbing (Harmondsworth, England: Penguin Books, 1939), p. 150.

CHAPTER 19: THINKING BEGINS AT HOME

160 *Nash's definition of a family. Family Reunion* by Ogden Nash (Boston: Little, Brown & Company, 1950). Foreword.

161 *Quotations from Gesell. The Child from Five to Ten* by Arnold Gesell and Frances L. Ilg (New York: Harper & Brothers, 1946), pp. 86, 186.
   Sex differences on tests. "Individual differences in ease of perception of embedded figures" by H. A. Witkin, *Journal of Personality,* September, 1950, Vol. 19, pp. 1-15. "Reasoning in humans. III. The mechanisms of equivalent stimuli and of reasoning" by Norman R. F. Maier, *Journal of Experimental Psychology,* October, 1945, Vol. 35, pp. 349-60.
   "Now, no fair thinking!" The cartoon appeared in *The New Yorker,* September 9, 1950, p. 78.

162 *Women and insurance. Women Never Go Broke* by Bj Kidd (Philadelphia: J. B. Lippincott Company, 1948).
   Checkbook anecdote. "My banking daze" by Emily Kimbrough, *Reader's Digest,* March, 1951, pp. 105-6.
   Women on juries. "The verdict on women jurors" by Gertrude Samuels, *New York Times Magazine,* May 7, 1950, pp. 22 ff.
   Women lawyers. See *Courts on Trial* by Jerome Frank, mentioned above.

CHAPTER 20: THE MIND FROM NINE TO FIVE

Page

166 *Manhattan realty transaction. New York Times*, February 4, 1951, Sect. 8, p. 1.

167 *Study of 100 successful businessmen.* "The business executive; the psychodynamics of a social role" by William E. Henry, *American Journal of Sociology*, January, 1949, Vol. 54, pp. 286-91.
Lord Milner. Pilgrim's Way; an Essay in Recollection by John Buchan (Lord Tweedsmuir) (Boston: Houghton Mifflin Company, 1940), pp. 97-98.

168 *Mathematics of business strategy.* See *Theory of Games and Economic Behavior* by John von Neumann and Oskar Morgenstern (Princeton: Princeton University Press, 1944). The quotation is from "The theory of games" by Oskar Morgenstern, *Scientific American*, May, 1949, Vol. 180, pp. 22-25.

169 *Decision-making.* This chapter owes much to *The Functions of the Executive* by Chester I. Barnard (Cambridge, Massachusetts: Harvard University Press, 1938). The quotation is from p. 194. See also *Administrative Behavior; a Study of Decision-making Processes in Administrative Organization* by Herbert A. Simon (New York: The Macmillan Company, 1947).
Frozen food. "If I were twenty-one" by Clarence Birdseye, *American Magazine*, February, 1951, pp. 19, 112-16.

170 *Sidewalk sanitation. The New Yorker*, March 11, 1950, p. 20.
Chicken in the rough. Time, May 15, 1950, p. 90.
Young's apples. "A fortune for your thoughts" by Jerome Beatty, *American Magazine*, December, 1950, pp. 30 ff.

171 *Ten cents a cup. New York Times*, October 22, 1950, p. F3.
Getting home. "The tests of management," *Fortune*, July, 1950, pp. 92-107.

CHAPTER 21: FREEDOM FROM ERROR?

172 *Popular errors.* The original title of Sir Thomas Browne's "Vulgar Errors" was *Pseudodoxia Epidemica. The Natural History of Nonsense* by Bergen Evans (New York: Alfred A. Knopf, Inc., 1946).
Galileo. See *The Origins of Modern Science, 1300-1800* by H. Butterfield (London: George Bell & Sons, Ltd., 1950), pp. 69-70.
Voltaire. See Bartlett's *Familiar Quotations*.
Presumption of innocence. See, for instance, *The Law and You* by Max Radin (New York: New American Library, 1948), p. 99, or review of *The Law* by Rene A. Wormser (New York: Simon &

Schuster, Inc., 1949) by Jerome Frank in *New York Times Book Review*, November 20, 1949.

173   *Gettysburg address.* See Carl Sandburg's Lincoln biography.
      Odds on heads or tails. The Science of Chance by Levinson (see Reading List).
      "Everybody talks about the weather." See Stevenson's *Home Book of Quotations.*
      Color-blind men in the air force. "Color blindness" by Alphonse Chapanis, *Scientific American*, March, 1951, Vol. 184, pp. 48-53.
      Schicklgruber. See *Columbia Encyclopedia*, 2nd edition.
      "Are You Educated?" Life, October 16, 1950.

174   *Where Do People Take Their Troubles?* by Lee R. Steiner (Boston: Houghton Mifflin Company, 1945).

175   *"Education to reality."* The quotation from Sigmund Freud is from his *The Future of an Illusion* (New York: Liveright Publishing Corporation, 1949), p. 86.
      Quotation from Sir Joshua Reynolds. See *The Diary and Sundry Observations of Thomas Alva Edison* edited by Dagobert D. Runes (New York: Philosophical Library, 1948), p. 166.
      UN report on Bolivia. New York Times, October 20, 1950, p. 15.

176   *Dynamic symmetry.* See the works of Jay Hambidge and, for instance, *The Geometry of Art and Life* by Matila Ghyka (New York: Sheed & Ward, 1946).
      Schillinger system. See *The Mathematical Basis of the Arts* by Joseph Schillinger (New York: Philosophical Library, 1948).
      Conversations, concert programs, marriages. See *Human Behavior and the Principle of Least Effort; an Introduction to Human Ecology* by George Kingsley Zipf (Cambridge, Massachusetts: Addison-Wesley Press, 1949).
      Emotional ups and downs. See *Cycles* by Edward R. Dewey and Edwin F. Dakin (New York: Henry Holt & Company, Inc., 1949 rev. ed.), p. 61 reference to studies by Professor Rex B. Hersey of University of Pennsylvania.
      Poker. See the book by von Neumann and Morgenstern, mentioned before.
      Mathematical biophysics. See the work of Professor N. Rashevsky of the University of Chicago.
      Factor analysis. See especially the work of Professor L. L. Thurstone of the University of Chicago.
      On Growth and Form by D'Arcy W. Thompson, new edition (New York: The Macmillan Company, 1942).

Page

177 *Voters of Sandusky, Ohio. The People's Choice; How the Voter Makes Up His Mind in a Presidential Campaign* by Paul F. Lazarsfeld, Bernard Berelson, and Hazel Gaudet (New York: Duell, Sloan & Pearce, 1944), p. 99.

YOUR PERSONAL INDEX

Add other page numbers you may want to refer to:

Index